Love, Play, and Magic
Business Reimagined

Love, Play, and Magic Business Reimagined

By Lauren Wallett

This book is dedicated to Leigh Wallett

This book, like everything else in my life, wouldn't have been possible without the constant love, encouragement, and support of the best person I know: my sister Leigh Wallett.

Check her out at **www.leighwallett.com**

This book introduces the paradigm shift from patriarchal to playful business.

Contents

Introduction

What you're about to read is practical magic. Each idea is customizable and easy to implement. You'll become more confident with your capabilities and ignite your own innate magic. You'll remember that you do have what it takes to be successful. Your business will become more fun than you ever believed it could be. You'll alchemize your heart of gold into actual gold and make money from your magic.

This book is the paradigm shift from patriarchal to playful business. It answers the question: how do you reimagine business?

Patriarchal capitalist business isn't the best option. There is a softer, easier way. And while 9 - 5 is officially dead, the privilege of working for yourself is a full-time gig.

This book is for people who don't fit into the status quo. It's for:

The ambitious self-starter *who wants to make an impact on the world and leave a legacy of love.*

The generous freedom-seeker *who wants to generate income and lavish their loved ones.*

And the magic-maker *who's ready to scale an interdependent business that's wildly successful.*

Over 17 years I've reimagined business with hundreds of business owners. Coaches, Consultants, CEOs and Creatives have experienced wild-fire success. From boring, suppressive, and stoic strategies to enjoying light-hearted, sustainable Super Bloom businesses. Their stories and the steps they took are the treasure map to guide you over the rainbow to success.

Albert, a mentee from Nigeria, says his insights gained were electric. He took the inspiration into his traditional corporate environment and transformed the productivity of his team through play. They got more done, had more fun and felt energized and inspired to pursue new business opportunities. This book will invigorate and delight you. You'll never need to force yourself through another boring business book again.

These are the ideas my client's have used to achieve exponential growth in their business. They've grown from $1K months to $50K months - *often in as little as 90 days*. But it's more than money, they're making up their own lives!

I promise that if you include Love, Play, and Magic in your business, you'll exceed your own expectations. You'll realize that it's possible to get more than what you want without having to work harder for it. Instead of feeling separate and alone because of overwhelm and worry, your business will connect you to yourself, others and the world.

You don't need to resist relief for a moment longer. Dive into this book with an open heart and mind and reap the rewards instantly. Turn the page to tune in to the frequency of magic. I'm cheering you on from the realm of possibilities where your dream business already exists.

Business Reimagined

This book started out as a simple framework to set up and scale a service business online. But it's turned into more than that. Because while it's true that I've set up, scaled, and sold multiple businesses, it's only in the last year that the way I've done business changed dramatically.

Before I embraced my Phoenix Magic Mindset to live a life of play, I worked. I was convinced that capitalist culture wasn't a cult. I sought out businessmen to teach me how to do it right. I craved security in a male-dominated world and wanted to belong where it felt safest, at the top. But their business rules belonged to a patriarchal paradigm that served very few and oppressed everyone else. It was also nonsense. A world run by mediocre golfers, who couldn't book their own dinner reservations was a disaster waiting to happen. Toxic masculine patriarchy would fail. I didn't want to stop the speeding train heading for a crash. I got out to reimagine the idea of business entirely. You don't have to hate the players or the game when you can dance to your own rhythm with the music you make up yourself. But it wasn't nearly as simple as it sounds.

Even though I'd always been a creative non-conformist, I still found myself falling into patriarchal traps. I swapped good-girl for good-wife. And then I fell into the good boss-babe trap until I realized I was still playing by outdated rules.

I was so used to power coming from old, white, rich men that I gave mine away by listening to them. I bought into the same bullshit again and again. Work hard. Always be closing. And the most insane one: do it yourself - even though they didn't. The fact that men who manage companies can't manage their calendars is one of the insane realities of incompetence masked with privilege. The whole idea of hard work is warped. Stupid ideas like 5.30 am wake-ups as premises for best-selling books. When mothers have been waking up at 4.30 am since the dawn of time but aren't considered working at all.

It was almost as if a business was "for the boys" and baking was "for the girls." It seemed gendered as if the only way to succeed as a woman in business was to behave like a man. I didn't want to *lean in* to patriarchy. If success meant my multi-faceted, emotional, and creative energies needed to be stripped and replaced with logical, ordered control, it wasn't a success. It was stripping. And I'm only into that on Fridays. Kidding. Pretending to be someone you're not isn't fun, it's painful.

I wondered when business had become pressure and punishment instead of pleasure and play. It seemed inverted. It felt like a trick.

When I reimagined my business, I stopped playing outdated rules in a losing game. I realized that the rules were so ingrained in my scope of reality that I'd mistaken them as truths. Even though I'd had success it was a constant struggle and slog and I'd tell myself, that it's just what it was. I kept going, exhausting myself to the minute before the clock struck burnout. It happened again, a few days before Christmas 2019. I had my final business book edit and was set to launch it before the year's end. I was racing through an endless to-do list between client meetings. Time slipped away with very little left to spend with my sister, visiting me from overseas, or my friends. I was irritable, tired, and stressed. The book covered all the basics to set up and scale service businesses online, but it was dry as a bone.

For a Creatrix who claimed a life that's delicious, it was dishwater instead of a double shot mocha. Not a tasty treat and definitely not a vibe. It was like I'd made something opposite to who I was. I wanted to prove I was sensible, rational, and logical because I somehow thought that I wasn't. But what if that version of the book just wasn't it? And if it wasn't it, what was?

My sister - also a business coach, asked: *"What are the three ingredients in your business success?"*

"Love, Play and Magic," spilled out my mouth without a second thought.

Effortless. Easy. Exact.

"Then write about that," she said.

Could it really be that simple? That straightforward? I'd skirted around the ideas but had never said them straight. I didn't think Love, Play, and Magic sounded professional and business-ey enough. I didn't think anyone would take me seriously. It was one of those, *"I can't say that!"* moments of insecurity and embarrassment. *"They'll call me crazy!"* came the voice of fear from deep inside me.

Cause here's the thing. I used to feel like I was terminally unique and that no one would understand me, let alone support me for all that I was. My "too muchness" oozed out of me and I couldn't seem to put a lid on it or a filter it or fit myself in. I didn't trust that anyone would be there for me and believed I was my own safest bet. Backing myself was both my strength and defense mechanism. Building my own business meant building my own life and taking care of myself. My early businesses were built on proving I could, instead of playing because I was allowed to. I was scared and so played it safe.

Even my boldest moves were timid for who I really was. I wanted to be appropriately authentic like Marie Forleo. And commercially creative so I could sell whatever it was I'd created. I loved self-expression that came with a round of applause. (I still love applause). I had my ACE up my sleeve and wasn't playing it. I preferred other people's cards in case I'd reveal too much and really blow it this time. And everyone would hate me and desert me once and for all.

Trapped in knots of fear around discipline and dominance, I struggled.

I've had to undo almost everything I'd been taught to free myself from business bondage.

It was because part of me still imagined business as this difficult, out-of-reach entity. Why did I ever think business would be hard to do, instead of a natural extension of my self-expression? It's because we live in a patriarchal society that's fixated on power instead of focused on play. It's why so many women in business speak about "empowering women" as if power is something that can be given. Creativity is the most powerful untapped resource you have, and it can't be taken from you because it's innate.

My various business ideas have always supported me but when Covid-19 hit, my business dipped into the driest spell I've ever had. Clients canceled and my business as usual stopped short. I panicked and started listening to every old rich businessman I could find. Podcasts, books, online events, endless conversations with mentors. Each piece of advice was worse than the next. Quick fixes. Silver Bullets. Step-by-Step fool-proof solutions, and blueprints. And the absolute worst *"Just spend more money!"* On the flip-side was praying before sales calls and magical morning mediations. I even did one "divine feminine empowerment" zoom session that turned out to be group masturbation. Not my vibe hey, not my vibe. Nothing felt right and I didn't want any of it.

I knew there had to be another way. Because I couldn't find an external example, I knew there was only one place to find what I was looking for. I needed to imagine what I wanted and create it.

I reimagined business and decided that my business would become my Sugar Daddy. He'd give me whatever I wanted so I could move to my beach house to write fairytales, drink coffee and create all day. And in October 2020, I packed up my West Hollywood home and moved to my brand new Hermosa Beach home. My business is my

Sugar Daddy and I moved to my beach house.

And initially, that was the name of the book: How to make your business your Sugar Daddy so you can move to your beach house. Because when your business is your Sugar Daddy you get to fall in love with your wild, hot, rich life. Delightful. Except business is whatever you want it to be. I related to the Sugar Daddy dream for business, but you may have another equally delightful idea for what your business represents to you.

Welcome to the pleasure zone where your business pleasures instead of punishes you. In fact, pleasure is essential to your business's success. Business Reimagined means you get to have more fun than you ever thought you were allowed to. You're going to make your business work for you, instead of you for it. It's business reimagined from a punishing patriarchal dictator into your hot, sweet, Sugar Daddy.

This book is about reimagining business so you can reimagine your life. You can make your business your Sugar Daddy or anything else you want it to be. You get to make it all up. In fact, the reason you don't have a business and lifestyle beyond your wildest dreams (yet) is that you haven't imagined it as a possibility.

When capitalist patriarchy says work because you have to, the new paradigm says play because you're allowed to. Play is your purpose. It's the result and the process itself. It's not a fixed destination but an endless cycle. It's enhancing. It's regenerative. It's the whole point. Play is enjoying who you are and what you're doing with others. It's freedom through absolute presence.

It's not about *"If you do what you love, you'll never have to work a day in your life."* It's that *"When you share all you love, **you get to play**"*. Getting to play is the dream. You're getting it. All that you could ever imagine wanting. It's like making love or laughing. It's happening. It's life as a lucid dream.

If patriarchal dictators like Gary Vee (Vaynerchuk), are not your vibe then you're ready for Business Reimagined, Sugar Daddy style. That's business without 5:00 am wake-up calls, cold showers, and the hustle and grind of "crushing" anything. Because success isn't about hacking life to do it right. True success is about living a life that feels like a holiday.

This book has my personal stories sprinkled throughout. It will give you a glimpse into my galaxy and show you how I came to believe in business greater than the patriarchal version I'd been force-fed. It offers you the way of PLAY, free from the pressure of perfection and conformity. It gives you endless possibilities through the magic of interdependence.

Think of this book as an unbinding spell, undoing all the knots of tension caused by the old rules of business. You'll get released into the new paradigm. There is a far more delicious way to enjoy the rich pleasures of business done differently. The good news is: it actually works. Not just for me but for hundreds of the clients I've worked with over the years. Whether they believed in Love, Play, and Magic or not. They've each reimagined business for themselves.

My secret sauce to success includes the three ingredients: Love, Play, and Magic. This book spills all my secrets of how to use them in your business to reimagine your life.

For the recovering perfectionists and A-types (like me) here's how to read this book playfully. In case you needed it, your permission to play is officially granted…

How to read this book playfully

This book is not a prescription to take. The only requirement is a desire to do business differently. You get to take what serves you and leave the rest. Some ideas you'll have heard before and some may be revelatory. Others will spark memories and new ideas in you. Follow the moonlit breadcrumbs and see where they take you. As you read this book, make notes in your journal. Use your journal as a space for ideas. Pause whenever you like and re-read sections if you need to. Or binge the whole thing in one sitting.

You're making your map of return to the core of your creativity. Remembering that you're love energy is the first stage of reclaiming your innate magic. Revealing your love through play is the second stage. Your combination of love and play is the revolution. That's when your magic is reclaimed. And from there anything is possible.

The book follows a simple structure of checking outdated premises with true ideas. It offers alternatives to the status quo. It shows you how to combine Love and Play to make Magic.

At the end of each section, take a moment to note your key insights for your ideas collection. At the end of this book, you'll have an ideas map to implement!

Sustainable business is sexy, and it's done one day at a time. You'll complete this book one page at a time. There's no rush. Take it at your own pace and go as fast as you like.

Birthing your business

Introduction

"I'm getting into business" is more common than the saying *"I'm birthing my business."* But birthing is closer to what business is because it's a creation. Part 1 is about birthing your reimagined business.

Business isn't an external task to do. It's an internal reflection to express. Business is the ultimate act of creation. It's conceptualizing something that doesn't yet exist and conceiving it into a reality to share with the world. You get to create something you love and sell it so you can keep creating more.

First up you'll prepare yourself for what's possible. You are the example to follow. You'll unleash your limitless potential by tapping into your imagination. We'll examine your red hot fears, ride what scares you and drop the shame stick. Then you'll activate your Phoenix Magic Mindset. To rediscover trust in your most creative self, you'll remember the sparks of genius you've already experienced.

It's time to embrace the Way of Play so you can become RICH without working hard. I'll shed light on bad advice from the tricksters so you can spot it for yourself and spit it out. You'll get to sidestep the cult of capitalist patriarchy and go your own way. We'll check in to make sure you're not caught up in business BDSM which feeds into capitalist punishment. Ultimately we're replacing old rules with new ideas. To keep on track to your Over The Rainbow success you're going to stop and start doing one thing. There are three ways to prove yourself in business and I'll tell you which the best way is. I'll wrap up birthing your business with a personal story called Salt. It's about the time I had big dreams but hadn't done anything about them yet.

Prepare yourself for possibilities

Have you ever wanted to be something you're not?

Have you ever thought I don't have the time it takes for success?

Have you ever worried about what someone would say if they saw you on a video talking about your new business?

Have you ever decided you need to wait to make it better before sharing something?

We all have a running list of subconscious beliefs that drive us on autopilot. We don't even know they're there because we've accepted them as truths. Like, this is just the way the world works, there's no getting around it. Here are some examples:

A successful businesswoman wears suits and stilettos. She has her hair perfectly done, her nails manicured, and paints her lips bright pink.

A woman in touch with her femininity dances sensually in her underwear, burns sage, and sighs a lot.

An online marketer is perky and positive. She poses with her dog and posts uncontroversial opinions online. She's always appropriate with her humor.

The only insecurities that are acceptable to mention online are:

Guilt for not spending enough time with the hubby and kids

Worries about quarantine weight gain

Embarrassment about lapsed resolutions

Confessions about sneaky glasses of wine

If you don't feel like you belong in the world of boss babe, queen, or slayer, it's because you don't. The subconscious fear that you don't fit in is because you're scared to stand out.

We hold ourselves back by believing there's a formula we need to follow. And there's a paved way to get it right. Because there is no leading example that fits in with your vibe, you stop before you've even started. But what if you're the leading example? What if what you wanted, doesn't actually exist because you're the one who's here to make it up? If you've ever felt a longing for something unexplainable, a missing for something more, a desire for an alternative to your current reality... then I hope this book reminds you that it's possible. You are made for more. You're here to have at all. Everything you've ever wanted is yours for the creating.

Your business, just like everything else, is an extension of you. It's not some impossible external to conquer. Business is the manifestation of your love for the world. And when you treat it like that, your business becomes a source of pleasure, play, and prosperity. By sharing who you are, you shine as an alternative example for others.

Red Hot Fear

Fear shows up in multiple disguises. It usually hides deep in the core of other expressions. Fear loves to wear a mask.

Perfectionism isn't wanting to get it right. *It's fear of getting it wrong.*

Control isn't making sure it's all okay. *It's fear that it won't be okay.*

Worrying about the world or others is a masked *fear that you're unable to take care of yourself.* You project your fear onto others assuming that they can't take care of themselves.

Hopelessness is *a fear that you're not good enough.*

Powerlessness is *a fear that you're unworthy.*

Not wanting to put yourself out there or be embarrassed is *a fear that you're unlovable as you are.*

- Exhaustion can mask fear.

- Numbness can mask fear.

- Repulsion can mask fear.

- Positivity can mask fear.

I used to think I was fearless. I believed:

No one can help me.

I have to do it all alone.

If I don't do it, it will never get done.

My fear was so ingrained I thought I wasn't afraid of anything. At the height of my fear (in late 2017) I did public speaking, made a short film, went on dozens of first dates, and hosted events. I was out and about on the scene, playing the role of a cool party girl. I ran multiple businesses and side hustles alongside a growing client portfolio. Once I wrote and managed nine blogs as one of the twenty projects I had on the boil. The truth was I couldn't stop because whenever I did, I'd feel overwhelmed with sadness. I was "on top" of it all. Buried underneath were feelings I didn't want to face. My fear also showed up as anger.

Denying fear is a double burden. Feeling afraid is heavy. On top of that pretending that you don't feel what you feel is exhausting. Denying your reality is lying to yourself and breaks your trust. It expresses itself as not trusting others and the world. It's hard to feel connected to who you are when you're not being honest about it. That's why revealing your feelings is a liberation.

You dissolve your fear when you shine the light of truth by expressing it. Red hot fear dissolves into warm pink love of acceptance. Revealing your fears is a personal revolution because you're inviting change to take place.

I recommend a therapist, coach, energy healer, or 12-step program to dissolve fear blocks. The first step is admitting you have them. Fear thrives in isolation so don't tackle it alone. Love it into the light through sharing it.

When you've accessed your fear, it's time to ride it.

Dragon Riders

I like to imagine my fear as a fire breathing dragon that protects me. I imagine climbing on my fear dragons back like Khaleesi in Game of Thrones. We soar above what's stopping me to get a dragon's eye view of what's going on.

If I stay on the ground in the thick of the problem, I'm stuck thinking I need to come up with a solution. I've thought I've needed a way out when in reality, I've needed a way up. Dragon riding gives me a perspective shift through my imagination. I recognize the fear and I ride it nowhere. Nowhere is the place to be. Nowhere is now here with space between. It's heightened presence.

Nowhere is the place to be.

Nowhere is
now   here
with space between.

When you expand the space between your reaction or response, you enter the realm of possibilities. It's the creative matrix of nothing and everything. The space of no-when. Instead of asking yourself what you must do, you imagine what you want. And then reimagine. You get there through dragon ridding.

Dragon Riders say things like: *"Write the book you want to read."* You can stay frustrated with the status quo or you can invent an entirely new paradigm.

Let your fire breathing dragon ride you someplace over the rainbow to the time and space after your problem is solved. Don't fixate on how that happens, focus on after it happens. Then what? Imagine what different looks like. Paint the picture as a full sensory experience. Visualize it. Taste it. Touch it and feel its texture. Let the ideas come to you and remain open to the unexpected.

"You can't read the label from inside the jar" - Michael LoBue.

I used to love this quote. Until I realized you don't need to read the label when you can invent an entirely new jam. You do that when you get a dragon's perspective.

The Shame Stick

When I beat myself with a shame stick for something I'm feeling, the pain is worse, and I'm paralyzed to move forward. As a person who's never felt safe to feel, I thought that feelings were a luxury I couldn't afford. Sometimes allowing myself to feel is hard to do. It becomes impossible when I add shame into the mix. I'll feel lonely, disappointed, or devastated and then shame myself for having the feeling at all. When I'm feeling bad about feeling, I know I'm beating myself up with a shame stick. And I get support.

Shame stifles me and stops me from expanding into the fullest version of my Super Bloom self. Shame shows up and I slip back into survival mode. I know I'm in survival mode when I don't want to feel. This happened with this book's re-write. Shame struck me down with insidious thoughts like:

What am I saying?

Does anyone need to read this?

Hasn't this all been said before by someone more studied than me?

Who am I to write this stuff?

Am I always living the Creatrix dream?

I know that if it's not feeling light-hearted, I don't push myself through. Beating yourself down when you're already feeling anxious or depressed is sadomasochism and we're not doing BDSM.

A reimagined business is all about pleasure so if it's feeling heavy, it's a sign that it's time to get back up and support. The magic of interdependence is the essence of what this book is all about.

You don't need all the answers to start. Let your questions guide you to imagine your dream outcome. Wanting a solution isn't the same as imagining what could be. We live in a technicolor multi-universe. You're more than just one thing and your answers are multifaceted too.

Imagination is your key to creative living. And creativity is the answer to every question you have.

Maybe you're not insecure?

A final idea on fear. Maybe it's not insecurity, maybe it's internalized misogyny? Ask yourself if the burden that's weighing you down is yours to carry?

Intrusive thoughts like:

- Anything related to your physical appearance

- I don't have the looks (or the right look)

- I need to lose weight first

- I need a better fashion style

- My hair is too thin/thick

- Anything age-related

- I'm too old

- I'm too young

- Anything related to "how" you think you are -

- I'm not interesting enough

- I'm too much

- I don't have what it takes

- Nothing is enough for me

These are lies the patriarchy has sold you. And they're inherently misogynistic ideas. Internalized misogyny isn't gender-based. The most outrageous idea patriarchy has sold is that creativity is feminine.

I'm not creative

If you think you're not creative, it's internalized misogyny. Creative is literally who you are. Everything you do and every choice you make is creative. When you remember that, you can start to get more c onscious about your choices. You'll start questioning your choices:

- Is there a more interesting choice to make?

- How could I be more expressive?

- What would a more creative option be?

- *Where did that choice come from?*

Well done, you've just tapped into your imagination. Because you're creative. *Drops mic* Thanks for coming to my Ted Talk.

Phoenix Magic Mindset

If you dream of a life that's bigger you may feel impatient that you're not where you want to be yet. A bigger life to you might mean, your own packaging design agency, moving to Hawaii or having a dog sanctuary on a farm. The further it is from your current reality, the larger the leap of faith. Just like a plane requires a runway, you do too. You're not progressing in a linear way, you're leaping into a new dimension. It can feel slow until take-off happens all at once. You've experienced a paradigm shift. The good news is that you started building momentum long before you realized. You've been in preparation your whole life.

Phoenix Magic Mindset is about emergence as your most magical self. And before that happens, you'll burn away everything that's holding you back.

Before we dive into the ashes to dig out your dazzling Phoenix self, I want to make this super clear. This is not a self-help book. Self-help is a booming business that sells the lie that happiness is a prerequisite for success. It isn't. It's not about feeling good or feeling ready.

Success is all about creating until it's created. It's about burning it all down until only the magic remains. Magic comes from action. Crafting, chiseling, shaping and remaking. None of this means anything unless you're prepared to take action. These new ideas need implementation. The magic seeker dives into the messy middle and does it until it's done.

It's not about getting it right. It's about keeping on going. It's about

- Building momentum

- Increasing resilience

- Developing flexibility to bounce-back.

Then when things fail, you don't quit before the magic happens.

Phoenix birds are mythical creatures that are forged in the fire. They rise from flames to fly high in the sky. They're the original trail blazers, blazing fire from their flaming tails.

Phoenix Magic Mindset is enriched by every experience you've ever had. Nothing you've been through is wasted. It's either integrated into who you are now or stripped away excess fear layers that held you back. The delightful and the devastating. Your trauma is transmuted into triumph with a Phoenix Magic Mindset.

Whatever has hurt and haunted you, plagued and gnawed at you are the flames to shape your rebirth as a Phoenix.

Your most potent self is forged in the fire. Rising from adversity is your beautiful rebellion. As a business creator, it's your magnificent defiance against the status quo of corporate conformity. You've dared to do it differently.

There are three stages to reclaim your Phoenix Magic and emerge as your most magical self.

Stage One: The Beginning

Your life starts shaped by your particular circumstance. At a certain point you realize that what you thought was keeping you safe was actually controlling you. Some of these safety measures were self-imposed. You tried to fit in instead of standing out because you were scared to be teased, bullied and made fun of. Or you faced danger and were scared for your life. You bought into societies norms and expectations even though the rules rubbed you the wrong way. You felt uncomfortable or afraid but thought you just needed to figure out how to do life right and it would all be okay. Until you realized, what if *this* isn't it?

Stage Two: The Burning

Your world starts to crumble. The foundations you've built your identity on shake you to your core. Maybe you're not who you think you are? You feel a burning desire to leave, start over and run away. You have to get out, but you don't know where to go next. You know that where you're going is nowhere you've ever been. You're on a hero's journey into the unknown and you face the dark night of the soul. Things get murky and you uncover new truths about the world, your family and yourself that you can't ignore. You can't un-know and unsee these terrible truths. Radical change is required.

This is the point where many stop. It's too much to bear, so they bury themselves in distraction, control and addiction. It's like the unloved wife married to the workaholic who starts popping Valium. She has an affair with the pool boy / her son's best friend / husband's business partner to distract herself from her misery. And causes herself more misery. When we don't address the root of the real issue, problems blossom like roses on a thorn bush.

But when you step into the flames, magic happens. Your suffering dissolves you. You're like a caterpillar in chrysalis, metamorphosing into a new version of yourself. You allow your former self to turn to ashes. It can feel like you're dying because, in a way, you are.

Stage Three: The Birthing

From the ashes of your burn down, you birth your new life. Birth is the ultimate creation and it's not limited to growing a baby. Resurrecting yourself is a rebirth. I've often wondered if you're truly a creator until you've been through your own resurrection. Everyone who has recovered from tragedy, trauma, oppression and suffering to rise again, has ignited their Phoenix Magic.

The beautiful part of Phoenix Magic is that it's not a once-off experience. It's never too late to start over and begin again. You've accessed your Phoenix Magic Mindset when you remember this. It can be as simple as getting out of bed to start your day. You commit to showing up to life as you are. You stop waiting to become ready or happy or motivated first.

You are right here, right now and are always at choice. When you feel the flames of fear licking at you, remember that you're being forged in the fire and your emergence awaits.

Quick Summary

Your beautiful rebellion of Phoenix Magic has three stages.

The beginning where you're plunged into impossible darkness of circumstance beyond your control.

The burning where it all becomes too much, and the pain engulfs you.

And the beginning where you rise from the ashes like a Phoenix, filled with magic.

Life of a Creatrix

Inside every entrepreneur is an artist seeking self-expression. Your business is an act of creation shaped in your image and likeness. It's an entity that's an extension and expression of who you are. The more connected to who you are, the more resources you'll have to grow your business.

We all have moments of inspiration, intuition, and insight. It's because we have an inner creative well to draw from. When we tap into our creativity, instead of running dry, it refills and expands. It's energizing, replenishing, and sustaining. When you activate your creative genius, you rediscover trust in your creative self. Your creative self is the heart of who you are. It's you without your fear, doubt, and insecurities. I call this the Creatrix. They're our innate creative life force. Your inner Creatrix is your mentor and muse. They've got the crone wisdom of your future self to guide you plus the sparks of genius to ignite your creative fire. They're exponential regenerative love energy.

You've experienced your Creatrix when you've felt:

- A burst of energy

- A flash of inspiration

- Alive, awake, and alert

- Curious to discover more

- Enthusiastic

- Ready to go

- Fully charged

- On it!

It's a high vibe feeling that fills you with joy. You glow with goodness. Like you've mainlined sunshine and are radiating star shine. You feel like anything is possible and trust that it is. You manifest your desires and intuitively know what to do next. It's like living life in the miracle lane that's filled with magical synchronicities. You're in flow with ease and grace. Things just happen for you. You're experiencing your Super Bloom self.

Ask yourself these questions:

Do you have millions of ideas?

Do you constantly start new projects?

Do you want to share everything you know, feel, think and do?

Do you teach others what you know?

Do you believe people change?

Do you see the glory and horror in everything?

Do you have your own life philosophy / value system?

Do you enjoy holding paradoxes?

Yes? You're a Creatrix.

You experience magic in the mundane. Ordinary activities become extraordinary. Life feels like a romantic, delicious, and indulgent treat that's made for your pleasure. It's delightful. Aliveness is an art and you're the artist. You catch yourself thinking, "It doesn't get better than this." And then it does!

It's more than you could ever have hoped for or imagined, with sauce, sprinkles, and a side of more! And you have capacity to take it all in. That's when you know you're in Creatrix mode. And you get to make it all up as you choose.

The Way of Play

PLAY stands for Purpose-driven, Light-hearted, Aligned to You.

P Purpose-Driven

L Light-Hearted

A Aligned to

Y You

The first business rule we release is "working hard" as a prerequisite for success. We replace it with Play. You Play when your impact comes from love and we dive into this inside the Love section. Business is a love amplifier. It connects you to a community and them to you through your product or service. When it's created playfully, it's a delightful experience for everyone to be part of.

Earning my first five cents

I'll never forget the first five cents I earned. I was five. I had a coloring book that other kids in my class didn't have. I realized that, if I traced the pictures, I could sell them and make money.

I told a boy in my class my plan and he said he'd do the same thing. It was my first "community over competition" moment. I loved having a collaborator. We met on the playground to do our first deal. As we were about to trade our money for each other's tracings, he said, "Both our pictures cost five cents. So we don't have to swap the money. Just the pictures." And just like that he blew my five-year-old mind. I thought he was the smartest kid I knew. Business wasn't just about making money. It was about creating, getting cool stuff, making friends, and having fun.

Growing up I forgot my first business playground experience. I bought more into the patriarchal version even though it went against everything I intrinsically knew to be true. I forgot that business is just an idea I get to make up.

How to get RICH without working hard

No trick, business is meant to treat you. You know that business isn't just about money but rather an enhanced lifestyle experience. Sure, you want success, but not if it means you have to sacrifice your lifestyle for it. You don't want hard, you want gentle. You want time out to read, to treat your friends to pedicures, and to spend lazy time laughing with your family. You want to be rich in all aspects of your life not just financially. Money isn't your primary motivator. And you want those around you to grow and prosper too.

Not only are you innately capable and generous but you're also ready for so much more than you currently have. And just because you can figure it all out, you know you don't have to do it all alone! You've realized you're allowed support along the way.

You get rich when you've realized that interdependence (not independence) creates happen-ness. And happen-ness means you have fulfilled your heart's desires. It's all happening and you're fully aware that it is. True wealth is choosing what to do with your time. You get to do life when and how you choose. So **RICH** doubles as an acronym for **R**ealizing **I**nterdependence **C**reates **H**appen-ness

R Realizing

I Interdependence

C Creates

H Happen-ness

It's not about Independence. If 2020 showed us anything, it's that it's absurd and ridiculous to see ourselves separate from the whole. We are ALL in this together and Interdependence is where it's at. Playing, loving, healing, and living together. What is the point if we get it all and we're all alone? We get it to share it.

Then we can take turns getting each other coffee and snacks. We're stronger and more successful together, not in isolation. We all hold a piece of the puzzle and complete the big picture when we come together.

It's also not about the pursuit of "happiness". None of us are truly happy if one of us suffers because we're all interconnected. We're grieving the terrific losses from the Covid-19 virus. The idea that we should just focus on individual happiness is absurd. It's like saying, "If I'm okay, it's all that matters anyway!" No one wants to be the only remaining soul, strolling the empty streets after the apocalypse. It's not okay if you're the last and only one standing. It's devastating.

The "Secret" (if by "secret" they meant a rehash of "Think and Grow Rich" by Napoleon Hill) is about the law of attraction. But despite this pressurizing "secret", happiness isn't a prerequisite to attract success. You don't have to feel deserving to get what you want. You don't need to smile at your reflection repeating "I am worthy" to get your desires met. You need to allow for the full spectrum of human emotion to move through you. That's vibrant aliveness. That's the heartbeat of humanity and the pulse of creativity. Happiness is one color of your rainbow. Give sadness a chance! I've found that devastation reflects a particularly luminous quality of delight. You don't have to limit yourself in only feeling certain things in fear of ruining your chances for your dreams to manifest.

Spot the trickster

I wish someone had told me who to watch out for, so I'm telling you now. When I moved to America, I met many men who've built successful businesses as mentors. My biggest mistake was listening to any of them.

The first hired me to do his sales calls. He sold $15000 programs which essentially taught you how to host a successful webinar. He promised a quick fix solution for coaches and consultants to make a fortune online. All you needed, he said, was a single focus of one high-end offer and you'd be successful. But did he only have one high-end offer? No. He also had a supplements business, a kombucha company and worked with his wife on her wine business. Like so many others, he sold the lie of single focus success, yet had multiple businesses to make money. It also wasn't a quick fix solution. There were 527 moving parts to contend with before you even got to making the webinar. As part of his virtual team, I saw firsthand all that it took to make the business work and it was chaos. It also didn't actually work. It was nowhere near the three-step plan he sold and, when I saw the truth, I couldn't sell his simple solution lie. I quit. Within the same month, he shut down the entire business and disappeared offline. Like so many other quick-fix, single-focus, copy and paste solutions, it was a house of cards.

The next time you see an Instagram ad listing all the things you don't need for a successful business, do a quick check. Count how many of those things the person has themselves. Usually, they have the majority of things they say you don't need. It's always more than just one thing because it takes more than just one thing to build a business. The pot of gold arrives over the rainbow and the path is multicolored. But it doesn't mean you have to color within the lines. Success is not a linear straight line. It's a kaleidoscopic rainbow and depending how you look at it, it looks different for everyone. The secret combination is adding your unique creative mix into your business. That's what you'll do when you combine your love with your particular way of play.

My next mentor ran an exclusive annual membership for old rich white men. The membership ranged from 25k to 100k. All were welcome but the vibe didn't check out. As an invited guest I had to sit downstairs and watch the event on a screen. During a virtual event, the mentor told me I should not have asked questions and only listened. It was like I was there to be seen and not heard. A token woman in the room. He preached connection but he was disconnected. Lunch was at tables like a high school cafeteria. Interactions were just as stilted and awkward. The membership promised peak performance, optimizing everything and leveraging personal networks. Yet I've never met a more exhausted, sleep deprived, frantic person. He'd call me from the doctor's chair between immune-boosting injections before personal training sessions. His days were time blocked, before his gluten-free salad wrap. Even a simple latte was a negative factor, said the books he read. It was all about productivity versus pleasure. Maximized efficiency and minimized sleep, for what? He seemed miserable, lonely and bored.

And every piece of advice I took from him was worse than the next. I worked for free as an opportunity to get paid - which was just free labor. It was crazy but I believed that rich men gave opportunities faster than I could create them for myself. They don't.

He introduced me to the self-proclaimed billion-dollar mentor who finally called me at 9.30pm on a Sunday night. This billion-dollar man, mumbled through mouthfuls of peanut butter straight from the jar. *"So sorry,"* he said, he was starving after not stopping again all day. Already in his mid 70s, he still didn't know how to slow down or stop. It wasn't impressive. It was robotic machine living and it was sad. If that was prime capitalist success, I didn't want it.

None of these men had the lifestyle I dreamed of. Activities that aren't wealth creation aren't a waste of time - they're life! The hustle isn't real, it's work addiction and that's a serious mental illness.

The best thing I've learned from all the mentors I've had over the years is what not to do and how not to do it. This book takes the cream off the top of the 10% of good ideas I've received and counters the 90% of bitter advice I've spat out.

The more I looked at the examples of masculine success, the more I realized how warped it was. Dominance, fear tactics, shaming, force and submission required for "opportunities." In case you needed reminding, working for free is not an opportunity, it's working for free. No man is your master. You are. So, the next time you hear an absurd business rule, take a good look at where it's coming from. Really take in the person who said it.

- Do they exude joy?

- Do they seem satisfied?

- Do they feel genuine?

Do you want what they have *on the inside*?

If there's a disconnect between what they say and what they do, mind the gap and don't fall into their trap.

If you don't have your dream job yet, it's probably because you don't dream of labor. You dream of life. Remember, if your only time out is scheduled, then you still don't have a business, you have a job. And if you're not in control of your time, you're a pawn in a losing game.

The cult of capitalist patriarchy

This is not a book about the pros and cons of capitalism, communism, and alternatives to social-economical or political systems. To set the scene: it is stating the obvious. The current system, which is capitalism, isn't sustainable. Profit at all costs isn't sustainable. Win at all costs isn't sustainable. Anything at all costs - cost's everything. Literally. Bigger, better, faster, and more NOW isn't about sustainability but greed.

The cult of capitalist patriarchy is about work. You're free to work! What a treat! Who doesn't want to work to survive?

It's sell or starve. Work isn't just what's most important to do, it's survival. When we're living in a warped reality of survival of the fittest through work, it's not about life or death anymore. It's work-life balance or death. And it's up to you to get that balance right or you won't win capitalism's prize: capitalist happiness. The cult is an army of happy workers, crushing competition to increase profits. Business is written in war terms because everything is seen as a fight, a defense, a battle, and something to win. "You'll make a killing!" "You're killing it!" Maybe you don't want to commit metaphorical murder to make money? And maybe the "it" the saying references, is your heart and soul? So what if these weird war sayings are cult nonsense? What if your winning wasn't the point? What if you'd already won? What would you do then? The cult only works when you buy into it.

Cults condition you to deny the truth of reality. They offer a definitive immutable truth. And they make all alternatives evil enemies. Cults are made up of victims who believe that the outside world is out to get them. So, they protect their cult at all costs.

Here's where it gets dark and creepy. Work is also linked to worth. You need to work to be worthy and you must do worthy work. That's not true either. Work as worth is warped. The capitalism delusion is that with hard work you too can be free. Freedom can be bought through working hard for your money. But the average rent in America is +$1200 per month and the minimum wage is $7.25. That means your 40-hour workweek won't even cover your rent. It's not about working hard. You're set up to fail. You need multiple jobs and income streams just to have shelter.

So what are the options aside from selling your time or selling your body? Become a coach or start an Only Fans? Join a pyramid scheme? The Magic section gives you multiple alternatives on how to structure your business to scale. None of the alternatives rely solely on the time for money trap.

The reason I don't teach old business rules is because the only way to win the capitalist game is to become the oppressor.

The only way to win the capitalist game is to become the oppressor.

You have to buy cheap time from people and exploit them for your own profit. There are alternatives to exploitation. An interdependent business model creates collaborative partnerships instead of pyramids. A cult serves the leader and the leader ain't you. It's a pyramid and you're nowhere near the top. The idea that freedom can be gained through hard work means it's a commodity to be traded. It isn't. Freedom isn't something you can buy. Freedom is a state of mind. Freedom is directly linked to how free you are to express yourself. The cult uses mind control to make you think you're free if you're consuming. You're free when you're creating. Creative choice is where it's at.

You know you're in a cult when "otherness" is taboo. Communism is the crazy ex-girlfriend to the gaslighting narcissist, Capitalism. And she was asking for it. Like those crazy Socialists and Marxists! Any reality that's not capitalism is a direct threat to the cult and must be shamed out. The cult's definition of normal is white cis-men. But the cult leader has a distinguishing difference. He's rich. The majority of men are poor like the rest of us. The capitalist carrot of *"You too can have it all if you work hard"* keeps the workforce chomping at the bit. Chomping for the chance to be free. Chomping and consuming. The majority conforms to stay safe inside the confines of the cult. Inside the cult everyone and everything is kept separate. It's because we become stronger together. When we collaborate instead of compete. Creativity is all about combinations. So we're cited against one another even though we all share the same oppressive leader. The pyramid structure means that some oppression is greater than others. The burden for some is almost impossible to bear.

As long as you're trapped thinking there is no alternative to capitalism, you're not free. There are always alternatives. When you tap into the regenerative well of your creativity, you free yourself. The way of PLAY (Purpose-driven, Light-hearted, and Aligned to You) is a disruption of the status quo. It's about everyone, not just some, coming together right now. PLAY doesn't have an end goal in mind. It is the end in and of itself. We're here to celebrate aliveness through self-expression. We're not alive to conform to some creepy cult. The capitalist cult is just an idea. And ideas change.

Let's get high

Holding hands skipping full speed toward the apocalypse is capitalism's bestie: addiction. The environment of capitalism is a disease breeding incubator. So, it's not surprising we're facing a tidal wave of addiction that's wiping us out.

The capitalism cult has Kool-Aid too. And it's marketed as glamour, fun, and something you deserve to treat yourself with. Especially if you're a working Mom!

Escape into oblivion isn't freedom. It's a momentary distraction. It's a quick fix. It's more silver-bullet solutions like miso-dosing psychedelics and ayahuasca ceremonies. Reality is just too painful for people to handle so they manage it through not being in it. There is an alternative that doesn't require anything external. You don't need to ingest anything. It's connecting to your innate creativity.

I come from a family riddled with addiction and lost my father to alcoholism. At the time of writing this book, I've been in recovery for over three years. Recovering the undiluted version of me has been potent healing medicine. But the cult will twist the truth to make externals the viable option because you can charge for supply. Freedom to buy at all costs! Even if the cost is human.

Asylums and psychiatric institutions medicate patients to subdue and control them. The cult markets addictions as success symbols and gets you to engage willingly. It's brainwashing. And just like it's impossible to come between an active drunk and his booze, you can't shake awake a "woke" drug addict. They will defend their choice in active addiction because they're addicted.

The racist war on drugs is another cult move to promote disorganized attachment to the cult leaders in charge. What we're told keeps us safe, keeps us dependent. We're disassociated from reality fixated on our work-life balancing act. And we're breathing capitalist propaganda with every inhale. *Namaste. Buy these yoga pants.*

The cost of living is all that you've got. Pay for food, water, land, clean air, shelter, healthcare. Work or die. People work three jobs and still can't make ends meet. It's not that they're not working hard enough. It's that the system is broken. We're doing more and more for less and fewer results like a heroin addict chasing a high. We're a work addicted society dependent on a solution that doesn't serve us. We're in bondage baby...

Business BDSM

Business BDSM stands for bondage and discipline, dominance and submission, sadism and masochism.

They're all the outdated business and marketing rules that are fear and shame-based. Business BDSM is typical rhetoric in "bro-marketing." It's not limited to men. Many recovering perfectionists lean into business BDSM in fear of "doing it right." You've seen it a thousand times: *"Crush Social Media!" "Slay your Day!" "Dominate your Competitors!"*

Although it's a kink term, it makes for fat-free vanilla business strategies. The whole "Us vs Them" ideology is boring and overdone. Viewing everything as a threat is terrifying and won't entice anyone brave. When you're appealing to someone's creativity, you're calling on their brave hearts. You're not convincing cowards. As long as you're bound up in knots of fear, you won't get anything done. A client who isn't a shining example of the results you promise isn't a quality client. Someone who doesn't get the benefits from your service isn't a customer you want.

If you have to trick someone to work with you, it's unlikely they'll go on to trick others to work with you too. But someone who chooses to buy from you will likely choose to tell others. They made an empowered choice and will shine as an example for others to follow.

It's time for a reality check. Have you been caught up in an insidious game of business BDSM? If so, you need to get out of bondage before we go any further. Because if your hands are metaphorically tied, then you'll be blind to the truth... let alone able to speak your own truth.

If you believe:

You don't have the right skills to make your business successful

You're not interesting enough for people to listen to you

You've missed out/it's too late

That there's a right way and a wrong way to do things

That you have to/must/should do certain things to achieve success

You'll never be as successful as someone else

You need to conform to a certain ideal to get rich

Business is hard!

Then you're in bondage baby! Here's how you get out.

Anything that feels like:

- Limitation

- Scarcity

- Fear tactics

- Flagellation

- Torture

- Punishment

- is a sure sign, it's outdated and not for you.

When you see the same old patriarchal sh*it online - scroll in another direction.

I'll share some more words the tricksters use to trap you in the Play section. If you get force fed advice that feels like dominance or pain, refer back to this checklist. If it doesn't feel expansive, it's not. Your business is about growth and expansion.

5 Ideas to sidestep the cult

The truth is you are powerful beyond measure because you're a creator. You are more than just one thing; you are all things. You are love energy trapped in human form and the way to remind yourself you're free is through self-expression. You do that when you share your heart. It's what the Love section is all about.

So, what do you do when you realize you're inside a capitalist cult? Aside from buying throw cushions because you're indoctrinated to consume, you reimagine post-capitalism. You don't get bogged down in all the things that could never work because they're built on the current crumbling foundation. You reimagine.

When I imagined what I'd learn if I didn't expect an old, established, millionaire to have my answers, I made up "Sugar Daddy business". You imagine an alternative. You reimagine business to reimagine your life. Here are 5 ideas to sidestep the cult and go your own way.

#1 Banish boring

Every moment is an invitation to celebrate aliveness. Make magic out of the mundane. When you add extra to the ordinary it becomes extraordinary.

Add extra attention to what you're doing. Watch the experience amplify when you do. You'll feel yourself fully absorbed into it like it's the most fascinating thing you did. Notice the details like it's the first time you've ever experienced it. The way the coffee falls from your spoon into the coffee maker. The swirl of milk changing your tea from black to creamy.

It's life as active meditation and it's like inhaling life force energy. It's energizing, invigorating and you'll probably feel high off it! Get interested in everything and not only will it become interesting, but you will too.

#2 Abandon the paradigm

The problem-solution paradigm is patriarchal and assumes you need to find the right answer. Often, you need to ask a more interesting question. Anything that assumes a paradigm is problematic.

Asking *"What's for dinner?"* assumes there's dinner. What if dinner was an outdated paradigm. A more interesting question is *"Are you hungry?"* Or better yet, *"What do you want?"* Maybe you'd rather pick berries in a forest? When I ask myself what I want, often it's cake so I skip straight to dessert.

When you're faced with a problem that makes you feel stuck, asking "what do I want" can help un-stick you. You may not need a solution but a paradigm shift.

#3 Burn it down

Starting over is always an option. You get to redo, do-over, and change your mind. You also get to dissolve. There is liberation in letting go. A huge part of creation is dissolution. There is purification through fire because only what is real remains.

Starting from scratch is liberating because it highlights what's essential in your life. You get to go back to basics. It's obvious who you are because of the choices you make again. You may find your internal creative fire shines brightest in some of your darkest times.

Anything that's felt like punishment is a practice to prepare you for creative living.

Your beautiful rebellion is daring to do life differently. Expressing yourself as an unexpected example. Overcoming adversity, recovering from hardship, and reclaiming the parts of yourself you lost along the way. You become what you've always been: a powerful and magical Creatrix Phoenix filled with firelight.

#4 Embrace more than just one thing

You're all the colors of the rainbow. Reflect all of them. As you expand into all of your multi-faceted, kaleidoscopic self, you'll reach some edges.

You'll reach uncomfortable places, like, *what if I was a person who went to Burning Man? What if I liked camping? What if I prayed? Stopped drinking? Took up a new sport? Exercised? Broke up with him? Left this town? Stopped going to dinner parties? Wasn't afraid to be seen and heard? Assumed it was going better than expected?*

What if you were a whole bunch of contrasting elements? You probably are. When you embrace more than just one thing, you'll shed layers of yourself as you grow into the new version of yourself. Outdated ideas will become upgraded. You'll change your mind. It shows growth and progress. You're not losing your mind - you're evolving. You know the saying - "Your old life, will cost you your new one." It will. Keep on.

You don't need to stay in places, with people, or around things that don't serve you. Learn to leave, again and again. Until staying feels like a dream you don't want to wake up from.

#5 When in doubt, add more you

No one will ever do you the way you do you. So, whenever you're stuck wondering what to do, think about what you'd love for yourself and do that.

Do everything in a way that's unique to you. Add your approach into the mix. How you do things shows your style and your vibe. Every choice reveals and expresses who you are. Trying to do life how someone else does it means you're constantly acting. And unless you're getting paid to perform, that's not your job to do. It's exhausting doing double duty, remembering the moves and lines of someone else. Allow yourself to do as you do and stand out as yourself. Your self-expression means revealing who you are and it's your ultimate liberation. If you're struggling with this, the Love section will help you access more of yourself.

Capitalist Punishment

Crushing is Exhausting

Creating is Exhilarating

Crushing is exhausting. Creating is exhilarating. Business Reimagined is self-generating and pleasure-making. It's the new era of creative celebration with freedom of imaginative expression. You get to shape your business in your rhythm on your schedule. It's all about creativity. It pours out from your heart and is regenerative.

Community means collaborating with colleagues and added support. You don't need to compete when you build a community. A community supports one another, shares resources, and thrives as a collective. There IS enough to go around.

When you stop listening to the outdated rules of others, you clear the channel to Creative Source. We're conscious creatures with free will.

We tap into our collective consciousness when we access our creativity. Complex means it's too big to do all alone. So don't do it alone.

Most old business rules aren't even conservative, they're just outdated. That's because they're based on a paradigm that no longer exists. Bizarre excuses like: *"It's nothing personal, it's just business"* and "work-mode" is a behavior bypass system. These excuses meant "businessmen" could excuse immoral, unethical, and unkind behavior. Because "Business" said so. But we're conscious creatures. Business is an extension of our conscious choices and intentional actions. Business is our ultimate expression, not a mask for bad behavior.

A compassionate business takes people into account. It includes dissolving systematic racism, misogyny sexism, heterosexism, ableism, and pyramid monopolies built on oppression.

The truth is, it's NOT that complicated. *"It's complicated"* is an excuse and a trick. Do you know who's complicated? Psychopaths. Caring people are compassionate. When you do business with compassion, you can't go wrong. Business Reimagined is a win-win. It's not on one-upmanship because there's no corporate ladder!

Much of what was considered normal work was compulsive and based on addiction. The insane counter to working hard was playing hard. But you can't counter work addiction with alcohol, drugs, sex, food, shopping, or any other addiction. It's all just addiction which is bred from disconnection. Instead of compulsive work, Business Reimagined offers clarified play. It's centered around connection. It also means you don't need to control others. You don't need to control your team, audience, or clients when you celebrate them. Staff and clients are attracted to a good vibe, not a negative one. It's not rocket science.

Prices don't need to be cryptic when they're honest. Prices should be straightforward, not hidden. It's not weird to talk about money - it's just a tool of exchange.

The old rules had all working to enhance one. The new ideas have one working to enhance all.

Old Rules vs New Ideas

Here's a quick summary for you. Read the old rules vs the new ideas and feel into them... which ones feel expansive and which make you contract?

Old Rules & New Ideas

Crush it	**Create it**
Competition	**Community**
Complex	**Channeled**
Conservative	**Conscious**
Complicated	**Compassionate**
Compulsive work	**Clarified play**
Controlling others	**Celebrating others**
Cryptic pricing	**Comprehensive pricing**

Stop this and Start this

For Business Reimagined, you need to *start* doing one thing and *stop* doing one thing. Stop trading your time for money. Unless you're a prostitute, you're not the product, you're the producer. If sex work is your work, by all means, carry on. But if it's not, stop selling your time.

A services package is not a discounted time bundle (i.e. get X3 hours with me for a discounted price). Time bundles are about selling yourself short. You need to stop that right now because the more that you sell, the less that you earn, and the more that you work. Crazy right? Your client's get you on the cheap, while you build up resentment and suffer the consequences. You're here because you're a premium provider and you offer quality, so stop seeking quantity clients. From now on, you'll only work with quality clients.

Do you know what trumps a King? It's the same thing that trumps a Queen: the Ace card. So, you'll start by playing that. Play your **ACE.** Your Ace is your **A**rtistic **C**onnected **E**xpression.

A Artistic

C Connected

E Expression

When you play with your ACE, your business will thrive. You'll create a sustainable, regenerative business. Your business will stand the test of time and keep your clients coming back for more. This is the only card you need and it's unique to you. We'll dive into this in the first stage when you establish yourself.

Pudding Proof

Business becomes easy when your results speak for themself. The proof really is in the pudding. And while there are three ways to prove how good you are at what you do, one of them is effortless.

There are 3 ways to prove to others how good you are:

- Tell them yourself

- Let others tell them

- **Show them**

Show them is by far the most powerful choice because your tangible results are undeniable. You're going to show to sell. If you really do what you say what you'll do, you'll have made it happen, and happenness will make you RICH.

Salt

At twenty-one, I was an unemployed actress. I had a Bachelor of Arts degree which (tuns out) meant nothing in the real world. I'd bought my first apartment with my boyfriend (whom I married at twenty-five) and needed a job to pay the mortgage. So, I got a job as a shop assistant in a home decor store in the mall down the road. After work, I'd sit at my giant brown office desk to brainstorm my consultancy business. I called it Salt and it never existed outside of my imagination. Salt was the exact essence of what I aimed to do.

And it hit me during Friday night Shabbas dinner. My favorite bread was challah, a sweet loaf of plaited kosher bread. Sprinkling salt intensified the flavor. Salt brought out the brilliance of the soft sweet bread and that's what I wanted to do for brands. I was the personification of salt.

I even bought a book: Consulting for Dummies to help me launch Salt. But the problem was, no brand worth its salt would hire me as the visionary creative genius I knew I could be. I wanted to be paid for my bright ideas, but I hadn't yet birthed any of my own to speak of for themselves. There was no proof in the pudding. I hadn't created my marketing agency (named after a dessert because *"The proof is in the pudding"*) yet.

I couldn't amplify things that didn't exist. I needed to bake the bread before I could be salt on the top. So, I baked up businesses to intensify them. I wanted to prove I could make things delicious. And that's exactly what I did.

Here's a key takeaway I learned. Instead of saying what you can do, do what you do and people will see for themselves. Live as a testament to your truth and you'll never have to explain it because the results will be evident. Instead of saying: *"Go all in on your dreams"*, actually go all-in on your dreams and people will line up to ask you how you did it.

Keep the conceptual idea in your mind and live into reality as the embodiment of the thing itself.

You can point to the light of truth or you can shine as an example. The first way requires you to catch people's attention and convince them to look in a certain direction. It takes effort and translation. The second requires you to beam. Radiating your inner light only requires you to reveal it. It's obvious and clear. When you show instead of tell, you blaze a path for others to follow.

So, if your services or products work, you'll be the first example of their results. You become the first example of your future clients. When you show, you don't need to sell. It's already done and that sells itself. It's not about convincing people that when this happens then... it's already happened, and so they know. Back when I was salt in human form, I knew what I could do. So, I did. Making it happen is how I got RICH and not just financially. I turned my ideas into gold - which is exactly what you're going to do next in Business Alchemy.

Business Alchemy

Introduction

There are three elements to your reimagined business. The first two are the foundation that you'll build upon. When you have those in place, scaling your business is almost effortless. The first element is how you create an impact with your business. The second is how you'll generate income. And the third is how you'll sustain success through interdependence.

But if you get caught up in every little detail, you'll lose sight of the big picture and waste hours spinning your wheels. My secret sauce to multiple successful businesses are three ingredients: Love, Play and Magic. And when you combine Love and Play, Magic happens automatically.

Business Alchemy is the process you'll use to distill the three elements. Together they'll form your reimagined business. The Alchemical term is coagulation. But you don't need to worry about how the process works. You've already started it in Birthing your business when you dissolved fears. Now we're in the middle of the process, the separation stage. And you already know the separate secret ingredients because they're the title of this book. Combing Love, Play and Magic will result in your Business Reimagined.

In this section I'll unpack Love, Play and Magic for you with practical strategies that are easy to implement. Remember to make notes in your journal for your ideas collection. Your ideas collection will form your strategy map to your Over The Rainbow success.

Here's an overview for you of what you'll get from Business Alchemy.

The 3 Elements

An **Online Persona** so that you stand out as exceptional to attract interest.

A **Growing Community** so that you connect to clients and customers who want to buy from you and share what you do.

Multiple Offers so that you have something to sell at scale to keep your clients coming back for more.

At the end of this book, you'll know how to:

- **Create** your Online Persona and

- **Grow** your Community to

- **Scale** your Offers

Creating an online persona for your business is key in growing a community with shared values. Personas are an easy way to access parts of your personality to express. Often, we recognize ourselves in other people or ideas before we recognize that we contain all possibilities within ourselves.

I saw myself in a benevolent Sugar Daddy who lavished me with treats. My pleasure was his purpose. And when I saw my business as something that wanted to give to me, I allowed myself to experience it.

Sharing the experience is how you'll grow your community. You'll create something others want to be part of and let them in. Choosing a metaphor for the type of environment you want to create is one of the short-cut strategies in this section.

Before you scale your offers, you'll need multiple irresistible offers. But don't worry, it's not more work to make more. You're going to tier and combine your offers you multiple them. I'll give you a full cheat-sheet to choose from.

When you focus on Love and Play, you'll make Magic without over-thinking and over-complicating it. It'll happen automatically. And happen-ness will make you rich. So expect the unexpected…

The 3 Ingredients

The three ingredients will give you three achievements. Impact, Income and Interdependence. You'll activate your Love to create an Impact with your business. You'll include Play to generate an Income from your business. And when you combine Love and Play, you'll experience business Interdependence that feels like Magic because it is.

- **Love** is about you.

- **Play** is about your community.

- And **Magic** is where you both come together.

Impact from Love

We start with how you wish to finish. With love. When you're creating a legacy of love, love becomes your ultimate strategy. You'll show up to share and trust that your dream clients know what's best for them. You'll build a relationship built on respect and connection, not shame and cohesion. Your ACE is how you keep your clients coming back for more. Your **ACE** is your Artistic Connected Expression.

A Artistic

C Connected

E Expression

You'll create an impact when you're able to translate what's inside your heart into irresistible packages. Everything you'll discover in this section will help you to formulate your future offers collection.

Break this #1 Rule: Work Hard. You don't work harder. You don't even need to work smarter. You're going to scrap hard and smart and share your ACE.

Income from Play

Play is how you decide whether choice is a do or a don't. You ignore traditional sales and let your clients come to you on their own. You'll show to sell. When you do, you'll position yourself as the obvious best choice and attract your dream clients. There is no competition because you're literally in a league of your own. Grow a connected community and you'll get paid to play.

Run all your ideas through this PLAY filter. Ask yourself, is this **PLAY**? Purpose Driven, Light-Hearted, and Aligned to YOU.

P Purpose-Driven

L Light-Hearted

A Aligned to

Y You

Break this #2 Rule: Always be Closing! Instead, let your clients choose for themselves.

Interdependence - that's Magic

Interdependence is the secret elevator path to success. It's about having a support structure that's built to take you straight to the top. The magic happens when you include others in your love. It's where one plus one becomes eleven. It's exponential. A miracle is just the unexpected. And that's what the space of possibilities is when love and play merge. It's the miracle zone or as I like to call it: the pure magic of interdependence.

This whole vibe can start sounding quite religious or mystical but in reality, it isn't. It's what's most natural to your core central essence as a creator. You don't need to figure it out, you need to remember it.

Business is not about screw it, or screw over anyone and just do it - yourself. You're allowed to have support, encouragement, and help along the way and you'll get there, faster together. You don't have to figure this all out alone. You'll get **RICH** when you **R**ealize **I**nterdependence **C**reates **H**appen-ness.

R Realizing

I Interdependence

C Creates

H Happen-ness

Break this #3 Rule: Do it yourself! You'll embrace interdependent support to scale and sustain success.

Business Reimagined is about abundance over paychecks and a custom-designed lifestyle. It's not about a 4-hour workweek, scheduled days off, and calendar-blocked holidays. If you can't take a random day off whenever you feel like it, your business is not your Sugar Daddy. Because your Sugar Daddy business knows that personal maintenance is where it's at. Your polished nails don't just do themselves!

PLAY your ACE to get RICH

As a flash-back summary, here are the acronyms I use in this book:

ACE stands for **A**rtistic **C**onnected **E**xpression.

PLAY stands for **P**urpose-driven, **L**ight-hearted, **A**ligned to **Y**ou.

RICH stands for **R**ealizing **I**nterdependence **C**reates **H**appen-ness.

Wrap the three acronyms together to get Business Reimagined like this:

PLAY your **ACE** to get **RICH**.

P Purpose-Driven

L Light-Hearted

A Aligned to

Y You

A Artistic

C Connected

E Expression

R Realizing

I Interdependence

C Creates

H Happen-ness

Impact from Love +

Love Quote

"People will forget what you said, people will forget what you did, but people will never forget how you made them feel."
- Maya Angelou

Love

I'll tell you a secret. Want to know what the greatest magic in the world is? It's love. This section is about how to access the art from your heart. Sharing your heart is how you stand out online. You'll translate the gifts of your heart into irresistible packages through sharing your ACE (Artistic Connected Expression). When you do, you'll have established yourself as the obvious best choice for your dream client. Without pretending you're anything you're not.

Your intention sets the tone for your love legacy. It's baked into the vibe of your community and company culture. We'll activate your creative genius so that you rediscover trust in your creative self and discover your ACE.

I'll share some of the exact questions I ask clients to create their online persona so that you can do it yourself. Answer them in the As Game. You'll drop the stress of defining a niche and, instead, share your heart out online.

Instead of fixating on your ideal client avatar and wasting time on market research, you'll focus on yourself as your future client now. We'll avoid the "Authenticity" over-exposure trap and build intimate feel-good connections.

And I'll show you how sharing your ACE means you'll never have to do sleazy sales because you're not selling. You're sharing your ACE. This section ends with a clients success story. It's what happened when she shared her ACE and sold out within a month. But first, I want to share a cringey story about me trying to act like Marie Forleo because, I thought she had it "right" and I was too much...

Unrecognizable

Before I established myself, I tried to be like other people. Pretty much the worst thing you can tell an actress is *"Be who you want to be."* And yet, that was the motto of the film and drama graduate school I went to.

My childhood can be summarized in two words: child actress. I knew how to act a part, but showing up as myself felt dangerous and impossible. "Me" meant trouble at home and school, but performing on stage was the safest I'd ever felt. Happiness smelt like a smoke machine and applause meant acceptance. A standing ovation felt like God hugging me. Like I'd really done good and, for the longest time, that was all I ever wanted to do.

So, when I got into serious grown-up business, I tried to separate my flamboyance from the scene. I did what I'd been taught. Check your competitors. Do customer research. See what people already want. The closest version to what I wanted was online marketing expert, Marie Forleo. I wanted my website to look like hers and even tried my own version of Marie TV, called "Malva TV". Unoriginal and uninspired but good, right? That's how Marie did it? It wasn't.

If a professional actress can't fake it, I can guarantee that you'll struggle too. When my "be like Marie" attempts failed, I redirected my efforts and decided to act more like a businessman. Enough with the pink and girliness. Maybe masculine meant more money? It didn't. You can drink with the boys and still not have a seat at the table. You can laugh off every innuendo and cringe shoulder rub and still get your bonus pay deducted. The point is not to become a better player, it's to make up a whole new game.

Back in 2016, I thought "stand out success" meant the old-fashioned way, like maybe when I'd been on TV promoting my book, I'd have made it? That type of credibility meant certain success, right?

In 2016 I went on national TV for my first book, Human Doing, and I didn't sell one. I knew how to sit, smile, and talk the talk but it was so stressful trying to remember my own script and fake "natural". I was acting as a version of myself but it wasn't even a sliver of me.

I never made a very good Marie Forleo. I made an even worse businessman. But I make an outstanding Lauren Wallett. The more I share what I love, the more I allow the world to love me, and it does. It's so much easier than I ever thought it could be. I'm not nearly as weird and misfit as I thought I was. Turns out I'm a boring garden-variety freak. Just like you.

But enough about me, let me show you how to access your ACE to stand out online.

Intention, Set, Go

Let's start with the end in mind and reverse engineer the process from there. So, first things first: How do you want your dream clients to feel after they've interacted with your business?

This feeling state is your intention and you'll bake it into the heart of everything you make. Tap into your heart space and feel into the gift you want to give them. I like to close my eyes, but you don't have to. I feel my feet on the floor, butt in my seat and hands on my lap. I take three deep breaths to center myself. Then I imagine the best feeling possible to flood through my body. You can do it to.

I want my clients to feel that it is *all possible*. So, I bake possibilities into everything I make. It sets the tone for every interaction I have with my audience. I serve posts that show how it's done. I create hand-held, done-with-you offers. And I share how I've overcome every obstacle to show that it's possible. Possible is pressure-free and doesn't demand perfection. It's about the willingness to show up as you are.

How do you want your clients to feel?

Condense it into one word. Write it down.

Your word is your spell, and you'll use it to make magic happen. Your intention (or word-spell) is your driving purpose. If at any stage, what you're doing doesn't align with this intention, you'll know you're off track and need to realign.

Now that your intention is set, let's go …

Love is your secret ingredient

To keep your clients coming back for more, they must want what you're offering. What makes your ACE offer unique is what makes you unique. It's all of you. As multifaceted as you are. We need all of your kaleidoscopic dimensions. You are the secret ingredient. You're what makes your offer so delicious and compelling.

To access all of you, activate your creative genius to get the gifts straight from your heart. You'll discover your unique blend of magic when you translate your heart's transmission into irresistible packages. Your heart is your source of regenerative creativity and your creativity is the most powerful untapped resource you have.

We'll infuse your dynamic creativity into everything you do. It's your slipstream to working less and playing more because you'll get paid to just *do you*. So, when in doubt: Add. More. You

Tap into your creative energy and you'll maximize and amplify who you are.

To be attractive, be attracted.

What turns you on, lights you up, recharges you? What are you drawn to? Notice what excites and delights you and keep a visual collection of what these things are.

To be interesting, be interested.

What intrigues, fascinates and compels you? What activities do you lose yourself in? Notice what consumes and stimulates you and keep a list of what those topics are.

To be loving, share what you love.

What do you adore, celebrate and enjoy more than anything else? Notice what brings you peace and satisfaction and do as much of it as possible.

Your love collection is what you'll share with the world. Let your audience get to know you and you'll draw in others who resonate with your vibe.

Activating your creative genius or discovering the art in your heart isn't about accessing the wildest parts of yourself. Yes, finding your edges means expanding into some new creative places - but it also means, rediscovering simple pleasures. I've always loved books and coffee but didn't think that was a fascinating fact about me.

Imagine if I'd known that I could make money just from reading books? And sell things when I posted pictures of myself and coffee? It would have sounded like some kind of Fairy Godmother magic. Yet, I have a podcast interviewing my favorite authors and they send me copies of their books. I post pictures and videos of me with coffee and my books practically sell themselves - on TikTok! I wouldn't have believed it was possible until it happened.

You are your own secret ingredient, and when you learn how to package love, your growth is exponential. Your ACE can be packaged into multiple different offers and sold at scale.

One of the personal assets I help clients cultivate is confidence. It's an innate part of my own Artistic Connected Expression. I package confidence training into multiple offers like:

Live with Lauren: How to Confidently Speak Live.

Pitch, Please: How to Pitch Your Business in a Minute.

Cinematic: Embrace your Star Quality to Stand Out Online

Stand Out: Activate your Creative Genius and Rediscover Trust in Your Creative Self

Flaunt: (This one's a combination package of all of the above offers that's coming soon)

Each offer is a creative repackaging of the same result. It's one idea shared as multiple expressions.

Activate your Creative Genius

You'll rediscover trust in your creative self when you activate your creative genius because you'll remember that you have all the answers inside of you. You're going to extract your sparks of genius with The Free Flow technique and the As Game. Combined, these ideas will ignite a self-generating creative fire to sustain your creative process. Your unique ideas collection will form your content strategy for community building in the Play section. And form your irresistible offers and packages in the Magic section. Return to these two exercises every time you need some fresh inspiration.

Free Flow

The Free Flow technique is about discovering the creative treasures from your subconscious mind. You're extending your stream of consciousness to stretch to an unexpected place. You'll leapfrog your way into a new direction from each word, without a predetermined idea of where you'll land. It reveals the unexpected or reminds you of what you already know to be true.

Sometimes the last word I land on surprises me as it reveals where my head is really at. Or I'll notice the contrasts and contradictions in the concepts. There may be duality or very clear patterns. How you sort through your free flow is up to you. I group similar words into categories. Focus on the flow, and then reflect to see what stands out.

Write down your name. Next, write what that word makes you think or feel? (it could be a color, a random object, a concept - anything) and then stop. Focus on the new word. What does it make you think/feel. And continue. Notice where you started and where you land. Hop to 8 - 10 words.

Here's my example.

NOTES

Lauren - Laurel - Wreath - Green - Recycling - Plastic - Straw - Sip - Coffee - Mocha - Love

From Lauren to Love

I realized that love is the driving force in my life. It's what I'm here to do. To give and receive love. It's an intangible concept so my next step was to make it tangible. How do I translate what's inside my heart? I share examples of what love means to me. And because the word before love was mochas, that was an obvious place to start! Pictures of me with my mochas. I get to share a moment I love with others. And it aligns with possibilities because it's a relatable moment that's very easy to replicate. Sky diving wouldn't be accessible to everyone, but luckily I love coffee! Start small.

Other words that stood out to me were laurel and wreath. It reminded me of a tarot card I love that has a sense of magic and mystery. It reminded me to add the unexpected into my content to keep it intriguing with layered meaning. So, I often weave symbols, colors, and personal references, into my style and stories on social. I scrapped "green, recycling, and plastic" because they don't relate to my messaging... yet! Maybe they'll spark some genius ideas at a later stage. And I have started sharing Instagram Reels of the ocean so perhaps it's brewing already...

The point is, you're able to take one or two ideas to start sharing and experimenting online.

To watch a video of me doing Free Flow in real time, visit **www.laurenwallett.com/biz-book**

As Game

These ideas add intrigue and unique insights to weave into your content strategy. Your answers will spark ideas for visuals as pictures and a brand color palette. Imagine that your business becomes the thing itself. So it's not about what color you like, it's about what color your business is. Imagine you wave a magic wand, and your brand becomes the actual title of the question. This is an aspect of its true essence. Answer as quickly as possible so that you don't over think the answer.

If your business was a ... *what would it be as a:*

- Color

- Aura

- Animal

- Car

- Flower

- Season

- Number

- Food

- Shape

- Superhero / fictional character

- Item of clothing

- Element

- Scent

- Sound

- Taste

- Physical sensation

Take some time to google images associated to every visual image you listed above. If you answered 'ice cream' to a question, then you'll google what came to mind when you used the word ice cream. We each have very different visual associations to words. You'll use these images to create mood boards for your reference collection later on.

I am the niche

You don't have to have a niche. A niche is like painting with one color. It's a cool conceptual experiment but unnecessary to limit yourself like that. It's another outdated idea that promotes conformity through categorization for consumerism. You're easier to target if you fit in. That's why it's promoted. Even though it's unnatural.

How could creativity possibly be limited into a niche? Creativity is unlimited, constantly evolving and adapting. Just like you. Sticking to a niche as a straightforward path to success is like telling a kid *"Don't grow because I don't want to buy you new shoes."*

It's just an old business rule that makes it easier to control you. After working with thousands of business creators from tech founders to artists to entrepreneurs, let me take a wild guess at what you want to do:

Do you want to leave the world a little better / kinder / more magical place than how you found it?

You believe in the best in people and want the best for them and yourself?

You're not here just to survive but to Super Bloom as all of you?

Great. Welcome to Aliveness. You're a creative being. You're the whole cake, not a slice. Not one ingredient.

Niches assume separation and difference. They promote demographics instead of connecting to people's hearts regardless of gender, race, and age.

It doesn't matter if you're a stay-at-home mom or a CEO - you both want to design a lifestyle and business you love. Your current position doesn't define your desires. Of course, you want to make money and be successful at what you do so you can provide for your loved ones and have time to enjoy life's pleasures! That's not a solution statement - that's called being a human on Planet Earth. Niches are putting yourself into a box because it seems safe. It's stifling. Despite what outdated marketers will tell you, not everything is about solving a problem. I don't drink coffee to solve a problem and I do it every day. It's a moment of pleasure, a ceremony with friends, a writing ritual and I love the taste. It happens to energize me and that's a bonus. It's not the point or the reason I choose it. It's an enhancement based in pleasure. Your product or service can be founded in pleasure and not problems. I didn't start my candle business to solve the problem of romantic lighting or to save money on electrical bills. Candles are purely for pleasure.

"I help people overcome something they're struggling or suffering with. I offer solutions" - so what? It's not about what you do or even why you do it (sorry Simon Sinek). It's about HOW you do. And how you do is all about YOU. Because *how you do* shows what happens next. It paints the picture of life after the problem.

How you do isn't about what your client needs or wants. It's about how you show up. You don't need to fit yourself to their needs and wants. When you DO YOU, they'll be drawn to you if you're a fit.

Stop wasting another drop of your gorgeous creative energy on trying to define yourself into a problem statement and express yourself.

DO you. SHINE all your colors - you multifaceted rainbow. You treasured diamond. You supernova. You're here to Super Bloom. Don't niche down. Rise in LOVE.

Want my secret strategy to success? I am the niche. I share what I love. I do whatever I love and I love whatever I do. Until I don't. Then I do something new. That's all. When you share your ACE, you'll stand out. People will invest in who you are and what you do. Pretending is draining. Expressing yourself is energizing.

When I opened the doors to my Performing Art School, I excepted a hundred students. The first month, I had one. The second month I had a class of four. I kept going and in two and a half years, I had over a hundred students and sold the whole school. If I had let my initial disappointment get the better of me, I'd have given up before I grew. The reason I didn't was that I loved what I did so much that it actually didn't matter that I only had one student. I appreciated the experience and what I appreciated, appreciated. Love helps things to grow. We all start from zero.

Every new social media account starts with no one following it. It always takes me longer than I expect to gain traction. If I hated what I did, I don't think I could keep forcing myself to do it. Love is the ultimate motivator. There's only so much white-knuckling a person can do! That's why turning every activity into play keeps the momentum going. Because when something is fun, you want to do it regardless of the results. It feels good. Love pulls you through, and play keeps you going.

You are your future client now

Here's the fast track to empowering others. If you want to empower others, live as the example. Not in a fake it till you make it way. In a 'share my heart out' way.

Start treating yourself like your dream client or customer right now. Give yourself all that you want and then you'll know what to give to others. Add more love into everything you do because adding more love is adding more you. More of you becomes more for everyone to enjoy. Your life as art and your work as love legacy.

I've worked with clients on Creative Alchemy (sometimes called The Rebella Journey). We rewrite their future through writing the past and editing their present. It's a fascinating and rewarding process. But what's been far more powerful is doing it for myself. Here's what happened when I did:

I experienced, firsthand, the value of what I offer. I transformed through my own process and embodied a fuller version of myself. Whenever this happens, I upgrade areas of my life. I've discovered books I had inside me and wrote them. My own capabilities were buried under my desire to help others realize theirs. If you're anything like me, maybe yours are too?

That thing you want so badly for others, give that to yourself first.

I've been training entrepreneurs to stand out for years. All the while, I was holding myself back. I didn't want to make it all about me and so kept the focus on them. They should stand out so they could excel. In reality, the moment I stepped into the spotlight and lived as the example, clients wanted what I had to offer. It is far easier to just do the thing yourself than convince people why they need it. When you show, they can tell.

You're the living proof. What you're about to create, hasn't been created before by you so you'll personify your business values. You are the living, breathing example of your reimagined business or reimagined life. You don't need anyone else to "get it" or be convinced that what you sell has value. You'll *get it* through living it. Your life is the value expressed. Your delicious life is the proof. Your business will give you everything you've ever dreamed of and more. When what you do works, it's obvious. You don't need to say it. You'll show it.

Forget the motivational quote and share the inspirational example in action. There's a massive difference between talking the talk and walking the walk. Of course, talking about your "best life" is easier. Doing it? It's a whole other thing. We don't need conceptual understanding. We need actual lived examples. SHOW through HOW you do life. That's leadership. That's legacy creation.

The vulnerability trap

Like "authenticity", vulnerability is a buzz word. It seems like every marketer has jumped on the band wagon to harness it for their own success. But what's being portrayed is generic vulnerability. Vulnerable stories like these:

I worked so much it made me sick, but I stopped that and now I'm well. Follow and buy from me.

I used to work in corporate and I was sad but now I'm my own boss and I'm glad. Follow me and I'll show you how it's done.

I suffered and now I'm living my best life. Follow and buy from me.

All the stories focus on overcoming a problem as a solution to sell. Because that's what traditional marketing tells you to do. You need a "bleeding neck problem" not a paper cut problem. So potential pain stories are hyped up, prodded and poked until they're marketing propaganda. Using suffering for sales is sick, sleazy, and it's overdone.

Moving away from pain is still not moving toward pleasure. It's just moving in a different direction. And we all suffer! It's literally part of the human experience. It's unoriginal and uninspired. There is nothing novel or unique about suffering.

A more interesting story is, what happens next? What happens when the suffering stops? What did you do differently? Solving problems isn't the solution. Stepping into a different paradigm is.

The art from your heart isn't your vulnerability. It's intimacy.

When you're able to connect with yourself, you're able to connect with others. It's what connects us to great art, music and dance. What we think of as traditional creativity is really just intimate expression.

My doormat says "Come as you are" which I love because that's what showing up is all about. It reminded me of Kurt Cobain's song with the same name. He was another tortured soul whom the world loved but who found it impossible to live on earth. He wasn't trying to be vulnerable with his pain. He channeled it into art straight from his bleeding, bruised and broken heart. And the world went wild for it. It wasn't neatly processed; it was shared raw and real and messy.

Vulnerability is exposure whereas intimacy is expression. You don't need to remember all the times you were vulnerable and share them. You just reveal where you're at right now. Show up as you are. There is no such thing as too much or not enough. You're Goldilocks (just right) for someone as you are. We each resonate with different things, but we can only reveal our own truth. Do that and others will resonate with you. The truth is more than enough. And yours is the most valuable asset you have.

Your love is for sharing, not selling.

Love as legacy

Traditional sales are often linked to seduction. And that feels sleazy because it's contrived and fake. Seduction is a slippery slope to coercion and rape culture. Thankfully we live in a post #metoo world and that whole vibe is simply not okay anymore. Not that it ever was.

You can't get away with seduction sales anymore either and you don't need to. Forget sales seduction and focus on Love as your lasting legacy. That's what you'll be remembered for.

You don't need to trick someone into something when it's the straight up truth. Trust your intentional feeling state and that they can feel it because they can. They'll resonate if it's a vibrational match for their desires.

Focus on the art in your heart and pour that into every ACE offer you make. When love is at the center of everything you do, it vibrates with the hearts of others. Traditional sales were about looking and thinking. Catching attention to inform about a product or service. This Tupperware costs $1. Get it here. Social sales are about listening and feeling. Here's the secret to successful products or services. They connect someone to who they are. Or they connect someone to others. That's the job you're here to do. It's the ultimate transformational benefit of any premium product or service. You don't sell that; you share connection as living proof.

Marketing your business is not like dating! That's a bizarre and outdated idea based on prostitution and ownership of partners. It's not a numbers game because you're selling to people not numbers. Every no doesn't bring you closer to a yes. That's absurdist binary thinking. Love has a gravitational pull. Get one yes and make another and another. With resonant referrals two becomes four, then eight etc. It's not a linear progression. It's exponential growth.

Impact Success

From unknown to established

Exhausted from waking up at 3·00 am to teach English to foreign students, she wanted to create a sleep-in business lifestyle for herself. She had a passion for Pinterest but no idea how to craft her passion into an established business online. This is how she went from a side-line business to center stage.

When we started, she was a part-time Pinterest Manager. She still thought she had to work time for money and that scaling meant group coaching or an online course. She'd listened to tons of podcasts, had a stack of business books next to her bed, and even done a marketing course. But still wasn't sure what her next steps were.

She'd bounced from one marketing must-do to another, but wasn't gaining traction. She wanted to be the obvious best choice for her dream clients - without pretending she was anything she wasn't. After hours and hours of posting on hundreds of Facebook groups, she'd managed to find one client but didn't know how to find more.

Silenced, in the heavy metal music of gurus shouting *"Do it MY way!"*, she had no voice online. Blended in behind the scenes, she had no stand-out social style.

Then she activated her creative genius and accessed her unique gifts straight from her heart. Her key insight was that she wanted her business to feel like summer. This translated into a bright, bold summer style. She transformed her Instagram from generic beige posts to bright multi-colors. She'd ignited her creativity. She discovered what attracted and interested her to share what she loved. And it attracted and interested her dream clients too. They loved it! And her engagement on Instagram jumped 520%! She got five retainer clients in a month. She repackaged what she did into group support and training and built a loyal following.

Instead of trying to be like everyone else, she showed up as herself. She gave live training videos that let her personality shine through. She grew her Facebook group to over 400 followers. (Now it's over 800 followers!) She stood out online with a vibrant social style. And fulfilled her intention with a promise for a brighter business through valuable action tips. She stopped acting like a background movie extra and claimed the spotlight to stand out like the star she is. She sang her own song on social and played to her own rhythm. And soon was top of Pinterest charts!

She established herself as the obvious best choice for her dream clients and within a month had a profitable business for herself.

+ Income from Play

Play Quote

"Why fit in when you were born to stand out?"
- Dr Seuss

Play

When you play, you'll attract your audience so they line up to work with you. When you've shared how much you love, they'll know you're the best thing that's never happened to them... yet! There's not competition because you're in a league of your own. When you play, you'll make more money than ever before. Play is about resonance. And resonance gets referrals. Your clients will refer their friends to you because there's a resonant vibe to be where you're at. You're a complimentary combination. You'll all benefit by playing together.

Ask yourself, is this **PLAY**?

Purpose Driven: Moving you toward your future client's intentional feeling state (Intentional)

Light-Hearted: Unbound by business BDSM and the cult of capitalist Patriarchy (Free)

Aligned to: Coming straight from your heart (Connected)

YOU: You and love are one and the same (Love)

That's how you decide whether it's a do or a don't. Put every choice you make through the PLAY filter. Filter to discover your own flow.

PLAY filter:

Purpose-driven

(Intentional)

Light-hearted

(Free)

Aligned to

(Connected)

You

(Love)

Play is how you'll captivate your dream clients within a growing community to keep them coming back for more.

I'm a start-in-the-middle person. The middle is where the money's at. It's what keeps your business going and growing. Before we dive in, let's talk about the parameters of play. By now you'll have an ideas collection forming your ACE (Artistic Connected Expression). This section is where you experiment with expression. We'll start off with some support for how to play your ACE. Next we'll translate play into a practice. What does play in the context of business even mean? This section will define what play is and isn't. I'll point out specific words not to use because you're not crushing competition, you're cultivating community. When you're clear on how to play, you'll implement the ideas and create a vibe on social media. Play is an action so you're going to dive in and do it. I've given you three powerful play strategies to enhance your play practice.

Welcome to the sweet spot. Now you're in the money, honey! You're making money through play. It's time for money talk. My last name isn't Wallett for nothing.

Finally we'll wrap up with a success story about a conservative lawyer. He's the least playful client I've had so I thought he'd be perfect for this section. Everyone benefits when they play more. He created a resonant vibe when he played to his strengths. And he made more money, more quickly than he ever dreamed of.

But first I'll share some of my own money-making-magic stories. Like the time I tripled a business and sold it in three parts. And how The Creative Business School started off as a creative showcase shop.

I'll show you how to grow your community and make money through play!

Magnetic Connection

I first learned the power of play when I ran my performing arts school for children.

Before I opened my school, I toured the country in Ladies Night as the only woman in an all-male theatre show. But when the producer ran out of money, we cut the run short and I was out of work. I vowed never again to put my livelihood in the hands of someone else, even if it was work I loved to do.

I looked at my own skill set as a qualified performer and teamed up with the choreographer of the show. We opened Fame Academy Holiday Workshops. We taught musical theatre to kids and I loved it. But I wanted more than a part-time profession, so I opened Star Quality Performing Arts School. I taught after school from a scout hall until I moved into my own location.

As usual, I had multiple offers: singing, acting, dancing, and musical theatre classes. During the school term, the kids came to me for Star Quality and, in the holidays, they'd come for a full week's Fame Academy. It was another complementary combination that showed me the power of community over competition. My school and the holiday workshops fed into each other.

I knew I held a captivated audience of students so experimented with other offers. I ran art workshops and then rented out space to an art teacher. I created a bath and body product range called Vintage Star with soaps and bubble baths. I teamed up with my mother and produced a range of kid's clothing called Rehearsal. I opened an Acting Agency division. I started a kids' theatre production company and produced shows for kids by kids at local theaters. I ran a birthday party company with entertainment and custom cupcakes. And more.

It was easy to up-sell each new offer because I already had a connected committed community of kids.

It was one of the happiest times of my life and I loved building and growing my business to reach more students. In under three years, I'd scaled different divisions to sell. I'd grown a community around a love-based brand and it gave me the platform to create and offer more. I sold the acting agency, corporate entertainment division, and school in one month. I retired to my farm estate to work on saving my marriage. The acting agency still runs in South Africa today.

A few months later, I did the same thing when I opened my Malva store. Malva's initial success was the community I created around the concept. I included different designers from all across South Africa into one showcase space.

Your greatest attractor is your ACE - your Artistic Connected Expression. Your internal magnet is your heart. After you've activated your creative genius it shines through every expression. The light of your creative fire draws others and warms them to you. When others feel your loving warmth, they'll invite their friends to be part of the vibe. It's all about creating an experience or environment that feels good to be part of. When you create a vibe, people invite their friends, and your community flourishes. It doesn't matter what the platform is, from a school to a shop, to a space in real life or online. Your platform is an aggregator. An aggregator is a place that links similar things together. The best part about an online platform is that you're able to attract a global audience. You break the barriers of time and space and your growth is exponential. And once someone has bought from you, it's far easier to resell to them again. For your business to flourish with less and less effort required, repeat customers are what you want. And that's what you get when you create a play space.

When you find people who want what you have, they'll keep coming back for more.

Play your ACE

Your business is your creation. And like sculptures, it's actually a relief to stand out. Michelangelo's David was always inside the block of marble. He just had to chisel away and craft it to reveal what was always inside. It took time, dedication to the process, and commitment to his craft.

It's said that the difference between a great versus a good painting is five brush strokes. And they're usually the boldest choices.

You'll never know what you're truly capable of until you put yourself out there and share your ideas with the world. Most ideas fail not because they're bad ideas but because someone was too afraid to share them. But usually, it's not the fear of failure that stops us, so much as it is the fear of success. Maybe you're just not ready for virtual coffee with Oprah or live Zooms with Ellen yet?

Every time you choose distraction instead of creative choice, you step back into the sidelines of your life. You are born as the main character of your life but sometimes it's easier to pretend you're not. It's because you're afraid of success. You're comfortable with failure, that's why you keep it around. Success scares you.

What's one step toward success you could take today? You're already reading this book so you're on track but remember - it's not about what you read, or think, or feel. It all comes down to what you do and don't do. Start by making some creative choices.

Take all your creative genius ideas from Free Flow and the As Game and translate them into your content plan. If you're not sure where to start **Create a Reference Collection**. Here's how:

Create a Reference Collection

Set time aside to scroll through Instagram, Google, and Pinterest. See what catches your eye

Look for images that visually stimulate, interest, and attract you.

Find and follow the accounts that you love.

Save images you love and make a mood board for a look and feel.

Note what you love and why you love it.

Innovation comes from your own interpretation. It's not about ticking off the trend boxes or copying someone. It's about combining elements you love into your own unique creation.

Still not sure what your ACE is? Write down your name. Make it an acronym so that each letter stands for something. Now you have a base for some additional self-expression. It's all made up and subject to change anyway! Don't take it too seriously. It's not serious. It's all just an idea to play with. It's light-hearted. Hard is anything forced. You want to create in flow. It's not a structured march, it's an improvised dance. In this section I'll give you simple structures and then you can go your own way.

At the end of this book is a Spotify playlist with a bunch of songs. I love creating with a soundtrack. Currently I'm playing "Little Shop of Horrors" on repeat. Fleetwood Mac's song: You can go your own way inspired this playlist because you really can go your own way. Listening to music is an excellent way to invite creativity into your life.

What Play is and isn't

Next I'll unpack what play is and isn't. Play is consensual choice. Play is attractive. Partying hard isn't play.

Play is a consensual choice

Business Tricksters give themselves away with the words they use. They want to control you, not play together. There's rhetoric and once you've spotted it, you can't unsee it. Fear-based people use force words instead of love-based people who use choice words. As a safe bet, anytime someone uses words from war - leap in another direction! You won't find peace there and that's what Business Reimagined promises. The problem with these words is that they can trick you into the tension of competition.

Play is a consensual choice. It's not shame or fear based. When you play, you don't force anyone to do something. Force tells you what to do. People who lead with force use words like:

- Attack

- Crush

- Conquer

- Smash

- Demolish

- Dominate

- Defeat

Choice tells you why you'd want to do something. People who lead with choice use words like:

- Embrace

- Get

- Give

- Grow

- Create

- Succeed

- Thrive

Force uses fear. Choice is based in love. Fear comes from a scarcity mindset that there isn't enough to go around. Choice comes from an abundance mindset that there is enough for everyone. You're not in business to land yourself a big fish. So you're not you hooking people, catching them, or reeling them in. You're partnering with people, and that means you both need to be a match for each other.

How do you attract your ideal clients? You don't force them, you let them choose. Show them your vibe and they'll want to be part of it. The choice to play with your clients instead of control them shows you trust them to make decisions that are good for them. You stop wasting time with sales psychology and redundant sales scripts. Treat your clients as equals with respect and compassion.

You don't need to trick someone into working with you when you're the treat they've been looking for. Play is a vibe. Pressure is not a vibe.

Pressure uses words like:

- Hustle

- Do it right

- You have to

- Work super hard

- You only get one shot

Play uses words like:

- Align

- Experiment

- You choose to

- Take time to rest

- You can always start over

A play space is a sharing space, not a sales space so you don't have to always be closing. You'll always be creating. You're cultivating community and your community becomes your collaborators and co-creators.

Woodwork terms are unnecessary. You're not hammering it out. Or nailing it. You're a creator, not a carpenter.

The truth is only brutal for lies. Truth is an exhalation. Words get twisted by tricksters to make the obvious seem murky. Feel into a word to see if it feels restrictive. The truth isn't complex. It is what it is. And that's obvious. You remember it.

Play is attractive

Attract your audience so they line up to work with you. Because they know you're the best thing that's never happened to them... yet!

Attract your clients, without approaching or self-promoting. Trust your future clients to make the choice that's best for them and let them choose you. Don't reek of perky desperation, so common in traditional sales. Here's an example of perky desperation. I posted on a Facebook Group, "I am looking for a life coach." The comments flooded in. Only one of these 146 comments said: "I am a life coach". The rest were perky desperation bombs:

- Friend requests

- Voice notes

- Long DMs

- Personal transformational testimonies

- Life journey stories (*I help, I'm excited about, I, I, I,me, me, me*)

And the worst, an overload of scripted questions:

- What are you struggling with right now?

- What are your hopes, dreams, and goals?

- For what purpose do you want a life coach?

- How long...

- I'm curious...

The theme was the same. The focus was on them and everyone was trying to sell me something. The difference is, when you're sharing, you're serving it straight.

Receiving all the replies was exhausting - and must have been exhausting for each person to do. It's also ineffective. No one wants something rammed down their throat. Quality clients are selective choice makers.

Ideal clients don't need convincing, and cajoling. They're compelled through resonance. You're drawn to your dream clients because you're a complementary combination. Your vibration is a match.

You'll attract your clients through creating a fun play space, that's inviting. Stop doing what everyone else is doing because it's boring, and no one cares about it after the fourth time they've seen it.

Partying hard isn't Play

In 2013, my typical Saturday was waking up hungover after hosting my themed club parties. Getting my latest guy of the week to carry my boxes of ceramic bunnies and frames to the market to sell. Spending what I made buying from the other traders. Unpacking stock back into my over-stocked apartment. Communal living with three to five other people to help pay the rent. Instead of a permanent shop, I had pop-ups in other people's spaces but, even with low overheads, I wasn't earning a tenth of what I had before.

I spread myself thin, and still, nothing I did felt like enough. So, I did more. Despite the fun, I thought I'd have, I exhausted myself. I'd swapped playing for partying and overcompensated working hard with partying even harder.

The problem was that I was escaping pain and not moving toward pleasure. And I couldn't tell the difference between the two. I knew what I didn't want but didn't know what I did. So, I did a bunch of stuff. I thought I was solving problems, but I was spinning my wheels because I'd lost sight of the big picture. It was more problematic than pleasurable.

I thought that if I loved it, I should sell it. So, I sold everything. I lived the hustle of life at a pace, racing to get to someplace else. I adapted myself like a human pretzel aiming to please. When they didn't want my champagne and sushi burlesque parties; I gave them cane and cream soda frat parties. Until what I did had nothing to do with me anymore. And when what you do isn't connected to your heart, it's the opposite of fun. It's punishment.

One of the worst pieces of outdated business advice is, ask people what they want and then sell it to them. I did that and ended up selling mimosas at the Sunday market. I was not living my dream. I'd shrunk myself to fit in and watered myself down - if you count vodka as water.

My heart was heavy and squished my energy out, scattered in all directions. I was still figuring out what play was. I struggled through the messy middle, sandwiched between knowing what I didn't want and wondering what I did. I couldn't decide if I was fabulosity incarnate or a wretched alcoholic who just knew how to throw glitter on things?

I see it all the time online. Busy moms celebrating suffering with wine as if that's an achievement for being miserable. It's buying into the old rule of working hard and partying hard as a balance instead of more of the same thing.

Play is connection to yourself and others. It's not punishing yourself so that you can get a reward. It's taking pleasure in everything. It's celebrating moments of life: fresh flowers, coffee conversations in the sun and creating things you love. When you add some extra attention to the ordinary, you'll heighten your reality to an extraordinary experience.

And you'll play all day.

How to create a vibe on social

A vibe is an emotional state or atmosphere from you that's felt by others. When someone vibes with you, they want to be in it with you. That means they'll spend time on your platform. Your posts are like party snacks and songs, that keep them hanging out in the environment you've created.

Traditional positioning is about knowing, liking, and trusting. And while you want to be a credible and reliable source, Business Reimagined gives more than that. You'll shine as a beacon of experience, strength, and hope so that you inspire your clients to take action. When you're positioned as a light, you'll guide the way. Before you've even spoken to new clients, they've had the opportunity to get to know you through all that you've shared.

Here's the thing,

- You're not just the secret ingredient of your business.

- You aren't just the maker of your irresistible offers.

- You aren't just your first customer.

You the combination. The sum of all the parts. The whole shebang.

That means you're the environment and the experience. Each sale is the sum of all you've shown and shared.

So, every post, on every platform positions you as either the place to be or not to be. When you're positioned as the place to be, your audience will invite their friends to your space. First, they need to feel part of something that welcomes and includes them. It really doesn't matter what platform you choose so long as you show up with all you've got.

Stage or screen, you position yourself by creating a vibe. A vibe sets the scene for the whole experience of interacting with your business.

You set the scene by giving your platform a metaphor for the environment you're creating. Is it a calm refuge from the chaos of life, like a day spa? Is it curated like a gallery exhibition? Is it like stepping inside a welcoming home? Is it like an exclusive party scene? Is it like a coffee shop? Deciding if it's a garden party or glamor rock concert will help you choose what style of content to share. Dream up the social gathering space. This is your play space. Make a mood board of elements to invoke the feelings you want to be associated with your business.

Now that you know the style for the look and feel and the tone of mood, you'll create a vibe inside the space. The vibe, like your ACE offers, comes straight from your heart. Fill your play space with what you love. It all needs to connect directly to you. If it's not connected, it doesn't fit the vibe. There is no room for anything other than elements you're truly, madly, deeply connected to.

Remember the PLAY filter. You'll get a real sense of what resonates with your audience by sharing who you are. Never ask what you haven't already answered yourself. Never expect your audience to do anything you haven't done. You're here to partner them, so neither of you can be part of a pity party or up on a pedestal. None of this *"Once I was a poor, lost, wretched soul and now look at me! Follow me!"* Just share your experience human to human.

Social Media is your best friend because done right, your audience sells for you and you can reuse everything you've ever created. Nothing is wasted and you can still get a high return on any past investment by baking it into a new combined creation.

It's social media not sales media

Imagine arriving at your friend's house and she tried to sell you a cookie? Weird, right. You went to socialize and you got a sneak attack sold to. Now imagine your friend made your best cookies and started to sell them as her business. You'd probably shout it from the rooftops and tell everyone. On social when you just share and don't sell, your followers will start to sell for you - if you treat your followers like friends and not potential customers. Social is about sharing what you love, not selling yourself.

Everything you've done up until now enrolls your community into a connected vibe with you. It starts when you share all you love. Your audience will self-select and line up to work (play) with you, because they want what you have to offer. They're magnetized by the whole vibe. Now you just need to make it easy for them to buy from you with clear offers and transparent pricing.

Playful Strategies

Strategies are just ideas until you implement them in action. So as you read these strategies, do them. Create posts and put them online. Build your business by building a future waitlist of clients. Then when you drop your offers, you'll already have a captivated audience.

The Cookie Strategy is how you make an offer irresistible.

The Queen Bee Strategy unlocks the power of repurposing content.

And **The Backstage Pass Strategy** explains why the mess you hide is actually your magic.

The Cookie Strategy

Can you tell I love cookies? They're such a tasty example.

If a visitor came to your home and you said, *"Hey, do you want anything?"* They'd most likely say, *"No thanks"* because they have no idea what's allowed or on offer. A million dollars? A puppy? A coffee?

Never say, *"Let me know if you need anything"* or *"Let me know if I can help you."* No one likes to ask for help. There are no parameters. It's too vague. And the pressure is on your client to articulate what they want and ask for it. You'll push people away instead of drawing them in. It's like those awful bot direct messages: *"Let me know if I can help with anything!"* I always respond. *"Yes! Please review my podcast for me!"*

That seems reasonable to me. It's the last time I hear from the bot/ coach again. Because they didn't actually mean they'd help me with anything, they meant, *"Let me know if you want to work with me!"* And we can smell fake, just like we can smell perky desperation, just like we can smell...hot chocolate chip cookies, straight out the oven...

Imagine you're a visitor and someone serves you a silver tray and says, *"I just baked these cookies, would you like one?"* Hard to resist, right? They're right there. Fresh! Made for you. Being offered to you! It's so easy to reach out and take a bite... Make your offers like that.

They wouldn't say *"Hey, would you like some flour mixed with chocolate, mixed with eggs, mixed with butter and baked for 20 minutes..."* Yet that's exactly what describing the features of your package, instead of the benefit is like. You also wouldn't say, *"Hey would you like a John?"* when you're offering a cookie. So, don't give your offer a weird name. Say what it is. Call a cookie, a cookie and people know what you mean. They don't care about the baking process. They care how it tastes.

And remember - someone's gluten intolerance or diet doesn't mean your cookie isn't delicious. It just means it's not for everyone. Because not everyone wants a cookie. Your job is to bake and serve. The right people will LOVE your cookies! And when you offer them one of your cakes - they'll be drooling for it!

The best way to sell is to offer the right thing at the right time to satisfy a hunger someone already has. It's never convincing them that they need it. Trust their desires. Create the environment they want to be in and then serve them something delicious.

The biggest reason people don't buy from you is that they don't know they can. It's not easy for them. So, make it easy for someone to buy from you with clear, direct, and exact offers.

- What do you claim you do?

- What's the result it gets?

- What's the benefit someone gets from the result?

Don't make them figure it out. Tell them how, why, when, and what happens next.

You'll draw your future clients in with the results, not the title of what you do. For example:

How to get three years of business growth in 3 months and skip 3 years of scale-up struggle.

Want to skip 3 years of scale-up struggle? Here's how to get three years of business growth in 3 months now!

5 secrets to get three years of business growth in 3 months.

New accelerator reveals how to get three years of business growth in 3 months!

It's true: You really can get three years of business growth in 3 months and here's how...

If they want the promise, they'll want to know the name of your package. For example: *"New Super Bloom Accelerator Program helps you skip 3 years of scale-up struggle."*

Then tell them where and how to get it.

Click / Visit / Apply / Enroll / Buy.

P.S: The Super Bloom Accelerator is a real offer. And if you want to know more, visit **www.laurenwallett.com/accelerate**

The Queen Bee Strategy

Your content works for you 24/7 even when you're sleeping. Your content pieces are the worker bees to your honey hive. You're the Queen bee sitting sweetly in the money, honey.

The best part about a content strategy is that you get to reuse your content again and again. And its value increases over time. Nothing you've created is ever lost. Every failure gets reframed into something that serves you at a later date. Platforms come and go. One day, Instagram deleted my entire business account. I had 12k followers and it was gone in a flash. But as the creator of my content, I have all my content. I can reuse it across platforms. If your strategy is about Influence through follower count, losing your Instagram would have devastating consequences. But as a content creator, it doesn't matter. You're not a one-hit-wonder. You can rebuild.

Based on your content genius, I've compiled some quick-win strategies to implement. Plus I'll give you specific tech tools to suit you. Take the quiz here: **www.laurenwallett.com/quiz** to find out which content best suits you.

The Backstage Pass Strategy

A ticket to a show is valuable but a backstage pass is priceless. It's coveted because very few people get to see behind the curtain.

If you don't want to be a fake and flashy, smooth sales operator, then don't just show up in the spotlight. Let your audience behind the scenes into your creative process. Show yourself creating and making it all up. Let them in. It doesn't hurt your image. It helps build trust between a connected community.

Breaking the fourth wall is a theatre term. It's when the performers defy the conventions of theatre. They leave the stage and go into the audience or address the audience, breaking the illusion created on stage. Break the forth wall of business.

Your not knowing, still figuring it out, making it up as you go along - all your "mess" is your magic. Show yourself working it out. Show to sell. Here's how it works. When you share what you do, you're selling without selling. Asking, "which book cover should I choose?" tells your audience you're writing a book without telling them you're writing a book. Show them ten covers and you've just told them ten times without annoyingly telling them ten times. Your not-so-subtle figuring it out is sales genius. You let them in on it, rather than announcing like a circus ring leader.

When you share your ideas as you make them up you'll get direct feedback through conversations. *"I'm making candles, what do you prefer? Do you like this label or this one? How about a coffee candle?"*

You don't have to be the all-knowing expert who has it all figured out. Share your process and your audience will be lining up to buy before it's even ready for sale. They're invested because they've been part of your process.

Money, Honey

Money is a tool for value exchange. It's also what we need to survive. But we can make it into an out of reach fantasy to chase. When money is made out to be an unspeakable secret, it's been given mythical God-like qualities. It's a lot of pressure on one idea to rule the world when Love's already got that covered. There are books, meditations, and rituals about money. It's described as a direct relation to your self worth or evil. So, let's talk about it to take the shame out.

Business is a cluster of ideas that when combined, make money. Until then, you're mixing and matching ideas and that is ultimate creativity. You know you're in business when you're making money.

Like money, business has become a separate entity instead of what it is, a connector. When business is understood as a creation, as an extension of the creators desires, it becomes a connector. It connects the creator to money from clients and customers.

When you remember that business and money are just ideas, you can start playing with them. They can free you instead of trap you.

Money Talk

When you're selling time, you're limited with the hours in your day and a capped price that people will pay you to use them. So, when you charge money for time, you limit yourself.

Let's break down a great case scenario.

$500 per hour for 8 hours a day = $4000 per day

/ $20000 per week

/ $80000 per month

/ $960 000 per year.

Great. Except:

Add 15 minutes between sessions

+1 hour lunch break

+30 minutes of admin for client maintenance

and you're at 15 hours of work a day!

That means working from 9:00 am till midnight.

WHO WANTS THAT?

And that's assuming you never get sick, ever see a friend, have any me-time or take a holiday. It's worse than a job. And how would you even get clients slotted in so perfectly? It doesn't work. But when you're producing packages, you can charge $1,000 - $100,000 per package, as they're not based on the hours you're available.

The Millionaire Myth

Millionaire mindset and millionaire's clubs perpetuate delusions about money. They tell you that the way to make your dreams come true is more money. Money is the only way to do whatever you truly want. Except that *having-ness* as happiness is capitalist cult rhetoric. It's not the point.

Life isn't a game of Monopoly. It's an experience of aliveness. The most valuable thing you have is your time. The capitalist cult has warped our reality to the point where we dedicate our lives to money believing it will enhance our time. We're drained and exhausted thinking that rest is life's ultimate luxury. Holidays and days off are our reward for working. Resting isn't a success. It's a basic human requirement. Time not working isn't the end goal, it's the starting point.

Tools are created to work for you, not so you can work for them. Money is meant to work for you, not the other way around. And if you're only trading your time for money, it's not working for you. So, if you're not trading time for money and you don't want to oppress others by making them trade their time for money, what's the alternative?

Connection is currency

The alternative to traditional business models is understanding the power of connection. It's not connected through customer research and asking what people want. It's connecting like an artist does, to your heart. When you connect to your heart, it's transcendent. When you know your truth, you tap into a universal truth. It's why Shakespeare's stories are still relevant today. They've transcended time because they reveal human emotional truths. When you make people feel you can move them to action.

If you can connect with others, you'll make money. Not because "your network is your net worth" so every interaction is some creepy agenda driven strategy. It's because connection is what we all want to feel. Connected to ourselves, each other, and what we do. It all feels meaningless without connection and it's not fun.

Creativity is connecting and combining things. New worlds are made and reality is shaped when ideas come together. Connect people to you, themselves and others to make more money that you've ever dreamed of. Think about it for a minute and feel into the truth of that idea. Think about the greatest artists, sports players, world-changing inventions like the Internet and services we can't do without. Notice how they're all connectors.

If you know how to connect through your artistic expression, you'll make money. Connect to your heart and let the love in. You'll live the life of a Creatrix and realize that you created your happen-ness. People will pay for access to you and every extension of you through your creations. We all want to feel part of something and, if you let people in, they'll pay you for it.

Let the Love in

Opportunities are everywhere. They're in everything. Are you allowing them in? The biggest shift I ever made was letting the love in.

I wondered, what if I let people love me? If I assumed they did love me? If people loved me, I'd feel safe to share my life with them. To intimately connect and reveal my thoughts, dreams, feelings, and ideas. When I let people love me, it's like I unlocked the keys to the kingdom and the world was waiting.

Connecting to others is just connecting to yourself. We're all so similar with our desire for love, security, meaning, and play. It's not complicated at all. If it starts to feel too complex it means you need extra support. Let people love you. Let them pay you. Start by loving yourself. Notice how you start to love others. You'll want to pay them for the value they're creating. Just like others will want to pay you. Experience the exchange.

When I decided to let people love me on TikTok, here's what happened:

I'd been on the platform for a year, hardly posting. After spending too much time on Clubhouse (the audio app for bro-marketing) I made an angry TikTok. It was about problematic white men. It wasn't kind and it didn't feel good. It went viral but the energy behind it wasn't loving. So I reimagined a world where every man wasn't a tech-bro into polyamory and psychedelics. I imagined that not every man wanted to mansplain business and creativity to me. I imagined that not every man would tell me I could introduce him to my connections and work for him on commission. And I took the viral video down. I decided to try something different. I showed up in love. I shared intimate moments of my day. From waking up and making coffee, to random self expression videos. I experimented, imagining it was safe to do so.

Two weeks later, on 11th December 2020, I reached 2500 followers on TikTok. Something had shifted. Two weeks later, on On 25th December 2020, I doubled my reach to 5000 followers. I set myself a "goal" (which is just an idea I hoped for because I had no control over it whatsoever) of reaching 10 000 followers in a month. I based it on getting 2500 each week instead of 2500 in 2 weeks. But on 15th January 2021, I reached 10000 followers and by 30th January 2021 (my birthday), I'd reached 20000 followers.

My growth was exponential and unexpected. I've been on social media platforms since 2010 and never had organic traction like this ever before. The difference was that I'd decided to let my audience love me. To let them see me and connect with me. And love energy doesn't lie. It's related to direct sales too. I've made money from TikTok faster than I have from any other social media app.

If this feels sticky to "let the world love you", you may have a few money taboos to address. Because money is linked to our worth, it's also tied to how much love we feel safe to let in. The two deepest human wounds are: I'm unlovable and I'm not worthy (or good enough). These two common shame sores may be blocking you from sharing your business with the world. Let's check if they are with Money Taboos.

Money Taboos

If you're running off money taboos, you'll refuse to make money easy. You'll be worshiping a false idol with a bunch of self-imposed weird rituals you think you have to do to get money. Write your beliefs around money. Do any of these sound familiar?

- Men make money

- Work hard for your money

- An honest day's work

- Money is evil / the problem in the world

- Stupid people make money

- I don't like money/money stuff

- I'm not a numbers/maths person

- Money changes people / is a corrupter

- Money doesn't grow on trees

- "That" (insert any idea here) doesn't make any money

Ask yourself if these ideas are true or do they belong to a black and white paradigm of this or that? If they're an old paradigm, it's time for a rewrite. Try this: "Money is an idea and I'm open to changing my ideas about money."

Staying open to change is clearing your channel to your creativity. Next time you have money thought, add an alternative into the mix like: what else could it be? What's a more interesting version of that?

- What if money was easy to make?

- What if money was fun?

- What if money was the least of your problems?

- What if you always had more than enough money?

Start imagining you've got the pot of gold over the rainbow. What would you do next?

If you can imagine that business is your Sugar Daddy so you can move to your beach house, you can imagine that money is easy to get. Your business *wants* you to have money. It's the by-product of what you make and share with the world.

Income Success

He maximized unknown opportunities

When we started, he was a pen and paper lawyer who had never marketed his practice. The idea of putting himself out there online repulsed him. He wanted to make more money but didn't think marketing would work for his one-on-one services business.

He was conservative, shy, and didn't want to appear unprofessional. He was used to working in person and then COVID-19 hit. He knew he had to keep his business alive by moving online.

When we started, he didn't know his true value was the gold mine of legal information he had. The gap was that people didn't realize they needed his services because they didn't know what he had to offer. When you're dealing with life, death, property, and taxes - everyone needs help!

If he got the confidence to share what he did, he'd be the best thing that had never happened to his clients... yet!

His ACE (Artistic Connected Expression) was his mastery of legal knowledge, so we used that to attract the right clients. No swimwear needed; he could influence with the information he had to share!

We used his existing email list and repurposed his emails on social media platforms for extended reach. From a digital virgin who didn't want to use Zoom with his camera, we did a live interview with an audience of over one hundred people. It was titled: To live and die in LA and his face was the movie poster! It was playful, inclusive and captivating.

He got clients from his untapped email list and built a business that wasn't marketing intensive.

- He booked four clients from his first email!

- He got 555 Instagram followers from only 3 posts.

- And reached his three-year financial goal within 60 days!

When I checked up on him a few months after we'd completed his accelerator program, he'd also paid off his student loan. His results were astounding! He made more money than he ever thought was possible.

= Magic of Interdependence

Magic Quote

"The whole is greater than the sum of its parts"
- Aristotle

Magic

Yours is not another's magic to make. But that doesn't mean you have to make it up alone. This is the part of the book where we combine Love and Play to make Magic.

Interdependence is the secret elevator path to success. It's about having a support structure that's built to take you straight to the top. You don't have to slog it out like the pavement joggers all alone. Interdependence is the secret password that gets you in the elevator straight to the rooftop of the moonlit party. Why go step by step when you could be dancing already? You'll get there faster, together. Interdependence gives you the support to sustain you throughout the creative processes of scaling your business.

Tadaa, just like magic:

you'll have prioritized your true values

let go of "busy work" forever and

have designed a lifestyle that feels like you're on permanent holiday.

We'll start with a very important idea. Understanding this is the only business strategy you'll ever need. It simplifies all the complex old-school business ideas into an obvious truth. If you've ever stressed about your niche, content plan, launch or roadmap then this is for you. Then we'll define what you can actually control so you can let go of the rest. I'll share what happened to me when I burned the candle at both ends. So you can avoid crashing because you're overly-capable. Next we'll look at exactly what you're going to give and what you'll get in return.

I'll break down different business models so you can customize a tiered structure of packages that doesn't burn you out. Planning your future back end offers will expand your front end offers now. I'll show you "The Over the Rainbow Strategy" so you master the messaging of your offers. I'll remind you to stop charging money for your time and how to package your offers virtually instead. Plus I've included some resources for instant tech support.

Then you'll get the support structures you'll need to sustain your success. Sistering and Bounce-Back are two of the best ways I've found to scale multiple businesses. Before you start hiring your team, you'll want to check your strategy to align yourself to success. I'll give you a Business Mentor Checklist so you can make the best decision for who you'd want to collaborate with.

Finally, I'll share an interdependence success story from one of my most dynamic clients to date. She realized that just because she could do it all, it didn't mean she had to. But first, let me tell you about my burn down in 2017. It's what happened before I moved to America and created The Creative Business School.

Ready? Let's scale your business like magic.

Seek magic

I reached a breaking point in 2017. It was my burn down year where it (capitalist patriarchy) became too much to bear. My corporate pregnancy lasted nine sickening months. Being awarded five major brand accounts seemed like a huge achievement for my marketing agency. But what came with it crushed me. It almost ended in a sexual harassment case against the global marketing director. But instead, I side-stepped the insanity and decided to make art with my broken heart.

I'd run my marketing agency for a few years and the results of my methodologies (and secret magic) had proved successful. I knew I could teach other creative entrepreneurs to do the same thing for their businesses, but I needed to lick my wounds first. Just because I could teach didn't mean I was ready to. I hadn't realized that, instead of just supporting others, I was allowed to get support to. I knew that something missing something. I wanted to stop pretending I was anything less than pure Phoenix Magic. I wanted to stop shrinking myself to fit in. I needed to make art from my heart. And if I was completely honest with myself, I craved the council of creators and visionaries who saw the world as it could be instead of as it was. So, I went to search for my people and took a creative sabbatical that landed me in Los Angeles…

Before I'd left for the states, I'd published a poem in an online magazine, inspired by *The Women Who Run With The Wolves*. Titled, *An Invitation To The Women Who Leave*, about my desire to seek out something I wasn't even sure existed.

And then, in a secret party, in a warehouse in Downtown LA, I danced blindfolded, with a hundred howling women. The hostess spoke above the drums, *"You heard the call, followed your heart and you came. Welcome home"* she said. I burst into tears of relief. I wasn't crazy. The rising wild, wolf women I'd written about were real and I'd found them! I knew that in this foreign land, halfway across the world from where I came from, I'd found home.

Finally, a place to put down roots to ground me and space to expand my branches further and wider than ever before. I took a leap of faith with the brave risk to stay in Los Angeles and started my life over again.

Two months later, I performed the poem on stage in front of the same one hundred women. I've added it for you to read because much of what's in this book comes from the devastation of my burn down years. You're reading the Super Bloom of those scattered seeds. I even mention candles!

An Invitation To The Women Who Leave

When spirit phone rang, I answered.
I didn't know that hello to myself, meant goodbye to him.
I bit the apple, tasted truth and thirsted for more.

And then, when the paralysis of patriarchal perfection was too
painful to endure -
for even a moment longer, I stopped…
doing the right thing
and did my thing.
Out the cage of corporate conformity,
contorted.
Into the movement of creative expansion.

The answer is art.

And now?
I revel in my perfuction.
My too muchness, my crazy, my truth.
Embracing the ecstasy and agony of this human incarnation.
My extra makes me extraordinary.

I am a woman who dared to leave.
The expectation, the have to, the should.
The good wife, safe live married to keep it under control.
Kept?
I leapt into the abyss of the unknown.
Because in my bruised, broken and burnt body,
in my blood and bones,
I remembered my way home.

From the seeds of discontent I'd sown,
that yearning of my soul's moan,
from the ashes of my burn down,
I, Phoenix have flown.

My reclamation of self is my greatest rebellion.
My revealing, a revelation
and my leaving,
a revolution.

To the Rebella, beautiful rebels
who dare to leave,
to overcome, to recover,
this is for you.

I am for you.
And we are not alone.

I was a rebel with societal validation as my cause.
Proving myself.
External expectation was the medication I chose
to meet my false with.
Busy bunny chasing dangling carrots.
Until the hole inside grew bigger and bigger
and it sucked, while I puffed and it pulled,
till I dropped in.
I am the wolf I feared.
Let me out!
The only way is in.
Follow your wild.

It's an invitation to the immersion of the inversion.
Our rebirth as free women.
And in the darkness, a celebration around candles.
Your light, to light up thousands more.
This is our transcendence.

In it, the ability to alchemize the lead of our pasts
into the golden liberation of our futures.
Collective transmutation.

And so it is:
We welcome the rising wild wolf women,
who left to return home.

Now

And now, just like Dorothy, I'm home and there's no place like it. I've lived a holiday life ever since. I've integrated love and play into the embodiment of everything I do. I get to share what I love and play all day and the results have been magic.

I've mentored business owners in everything you've read in this book and created The Creative Business School. If Fame Academy and Hogwarts had a baby, it would be The Creative Business School. It's a place of love, play, and magic that is equal parts educational and entertaining. We dive right into the messy middle and start with play, in a way that's nurturing, encouraging and supportive. I created what I wished I could have had.

Business owners come to thrive in all areas of their life. I have a Content Creators Council with some of the most brilliant entrepreneurs in the world. And I mentor business owners in reimagining their business to get rich in all aspects of their life.

I live an enchanted life in my Hermosa Beach home, playing all day. And thanks to my online business, I make money while I sleep. Enchanted lifestyle design and elevated business pleasure are possible. It's Business Reimagined that seems like magic because it is.

You don't need to muddle through the messy middle as long as I did. You get to skip straight to pleasure. Tadaa! From business to a beach house, just like that! You get to make your business your Sugar Daddy or anything you want it to be to serve you. And I'm here to support you on your adventure if that's what you want.

The only strategy you need

There is only one strategy you need. Ideas in action. And that's what Creativity is. Try an idea. Try another. Combine a few. Until you find your unique formula. Ideas come from your Artistic Creative Expression. Ideas that come from your heart are love in action.

- A niche is an idea

- Content are ideas

- A launch is an idea with a date attached

- A roadmap is ideas on a timeline

- A strategy is a bunch of ideas to try

Let's take the complication out of launching your business because it's not complex. Write down today's date. Write down the date in 3 months. What do you want to have happened by that date? Attach numbers to the outcomes, like launch my candle business with X2 candle scents. Plot 3 - 5 milestones between now and then to keep you on track. Under each milestone, list your to-dos. Well done. You have a launch strategy.

It takes ten minutes. And you can refine as you go. Replace ideas that aren't working and double down on ones that are. A strategy is just a step-by-step ideas list in chronological order. Don't overcomplicate it.

Process and outcome goals

Here's how to set goals that you can actually accomplish that won't stress you out. An outcome goal is a direct result, like: enroll three new clients. It puts a lot of pressure on you and you actually can't control the outcome. An outcome goal relies on the decisions of others. When you're obsessed with outcomes, you're trapped thinking you can control more than what's humanly possible. Control is a nasty trick. You think control works for you, but you work for it! It's outdated and patriarchal. Here's an alternative.

A process goal is something you'll commit to like: go live on Instagram every day. This is something you can control because it's up to you. You don't know what the results will be but you can do your part and show up to commit to the process. You'll feel proud of doing what you said you'd do instead of discouraged that it didn't work out as you'd planned. Your business is a creative process and it's made up of combining multiple ideas. They're all just ideas: your offer, your launch, your nurture sequence. Remember, it's not about getting it right, it's about keeping it going.

As a rebellious A-type, I love to set outcome goals. Because sometimes I want to control the universe with sheer will and determination. So I don't quit until it's DONE. But when it is, I often feel empty because it doesn't feel like enough so I set a new goal. When I focus on process goals, I'm encouraged by the progress I make on the journey. I feel far more satisfied because the results are my own! My business is my business and I can only ever do my part. The rest is up to everyone else and isn't my business to worry about. If you're anything like me, I hope this helps you ease into alternative goal setting.

For unlimited business ideas, subscribe to my blog:

www.laurenwallett.com/blog Start with the treasure mapping blog.

Burning the candle at both ends

For a few years, I traveled the world running my Marketing Agency. But then I got an opportunity with a global conglomerate and it was irresistible to me. If I could prove my methodology to them, I would have created a whole new genre of an agency model. And the results were incredible, but they were also irrelevant because no one cared.

My days were soon consumed with pointless meetings about demographics and busy moms aged 25 - 45. Every product from tomato sauce to frozen pies offered the same result: saving money and giving time back to busy people. It was obviously untrue but that was irrelevant. An actual solution required an entirely new paradigm reset, not another product. But marketing isn't about world-building. Business is, and I was in the wrong one. I felt like I was talking to a bunch of robots who'd never spoken to a human before. My life was being sucked out of me in slow motion. No innovation, transformation, or creative strategy. Everything was plotted months in advance and was beyond boring. It also didn't match the dynamic speed of the world but as long as we stuck to the set schedule, who cared? I was sick and tired of the toxic masculine culture. I was a business owner but treated as an employee. Corporate seemed slow, labored, and bizarre. Besides, I've always been more Caribbean than Water-Cooler.

And so, like my husband, Corporate and I had irreconcilable differences. I still don't get why a decision that takes a conversation needs a PowerPoint presentation? And while the money was good, being client bound is the same as being job bound, and I didn't want any binding. Money isn't my primary motivator. I wanted more than security. And I was fully over sleaze-ball clients. *"When you look like that and open your mouth and actually have something to say - girl you can sit in my boardroom any day!"* Compromising yourself in business isn't "how you play the game." It's compromising yourself and that's not full vibrant creative living. I wanted to share what I loved, a holiday lifestyle, and a community that supported my vision and values. I wanted more.

My version of more included:

- Lifestyle Pleasure

- Financial Freedom

- Creative Play and

- the opportunity to Make an Impact in the world

I just didn't know how to get it all yet...

Another "almost" mentor of mine was an old author who wrote about the dangers of a doer mindset in business. He was another in a long list who've lied about wanting to help me succeed in business when the truth was, he wanted help. Futile discussions that end up in, *"Why don't you work on commission for me?"* Oppressors love to exchange oppression for the word "opportunity." So, check out the next "opportunity" presented as beneficial to you or the person offering it. This man preached the benefit of becoming a manager over every other role in business. Delegation is what being CEO is all about - or is it actually the pyramid work style that only suits the chief in charge? That's the old paradigm right there and there's a sweeter way.

The worst thing I did when I scaled my business fast was hiring a team to do the work I loved. As my performing art school grew and I expanded streams of income into their own sub-businesses, I hired help. Soon I did the paperwork and pay role while my teachers taught my classes. I became the managing director of the school and I hated it. The more money I made, the more money I spent to keep it going. Until the sweet spot of my profit equaled the same as when I had a smaller school and taught the classes myself. I sold the school because the joy had been delegated out of the experience for me.

I made the same mistake a second time when I grew my team for my Malva shop. While on holiday, chaos ensued in the store and there was nothing I could do from so far away. Eventually, my mother had to fly in to sit at the store for me while I stressed myself on the other side of the world. The emotional price was too much to bear and wasn't the business I wanted to be in.

Here's the thing about an optimized business. It's not about bigger is better, faster, and more. It's about the sweet spot of the least effort for the most return. Doing what feels the most fun and makes the biggest difference. Business Reimagined is play that doesn't drain you but replenishes and revitalizes you. You want to do what you do because it's Purpose-Driven, Light-Hearted, and Aligned to You. You may only need three clients for your optimized business. It's all about finding your sweet spot and enjoying the interdependence of your ultimate support system. Even though I ran my businesses with independent contractors, it wasn't the support I needed.

As I've scaled The Creative Business School, I've done it differently. I'm in support groups. I've had life, business, and spiritual coaches and I get direct feedback from my dynamic community. After years of struggling alone, and trying to do it all myself, I'm finally confident enough to ask for help. There is only strength to gain from support.

I deliver results at scale through tiered offers, so I maximize my impact with minimal effort on my part. I've always loved working with people but now audition each client to ensure we're a match before we start. And the resonance we have gets me referrals and allows me to leverage my clients in my own personal network. With the right systems and tech tools in place, I virtualize intelligently. I make money while I sleep and I have lots of time to sleep!

My optimized business has a higher purpose than just making me money. It supports my holiday lifestyle. It allows me the freedom to create what I love when I want to. Whether that's volleyball lessons, candle making, planting, or singing show tunes. I get to design my day and customize it to suit myself. So do you.

Impostors and Creators

Some businesses inform and others aim to transform but most regurgitate. A photocopied version of someone else's oil painting will never be as valuable. Even if you're more of a collector and curator of ideas, the way you combine them reflects your unique creative expression. Imposter Syndrome comes from feeling like you're faking it. If you're feeling like an imposter, maybe it's because you are?

Are you pretending to know more than you do? To act like you have it all figured out so that you'll be taken seriously? Thinking you'll just wing it with no confidence? Are you trying to take the leap of faith to fly without building momentum on the runway first?

Instead of worrying about being an imposter, get the support you need to feel secure enough to take action. You may need to study, hire help, and practice what you preach. When you're focused on the creative process, it's impossible to feel like an imposter because you're taking action and sharing the process. You're a creator. There's nothing to fake because it's all happening on display for others to see. The results are tangible. When you share how you do something with others, it's real. If you don't know what you think or believe or stand for, you need to reconnect to your heart so that you do.

Three steps to overcome imposter syndrome

#1 Reconnect to who you are through what you love to do.

Start by remembering all the things that gave you joy as a child.

#2 Reclaim parts of yourself that you've left behind or lost in the past.

What aspects have you toned down, drowned out, muted, or covered up?

#3 Reveal those parts of your personality to regain your confidence.

Share who you are by how you do you, not how you act like everyone else.

Give

You can have the most brilliant business in the whole wide world. But if no one knows about it, it actually doesn't matter. It doesn't matter if you've already invested thousands of dollars in building your business. It doesn't matter if you're a trained and certified expert. It doesn't matter how qualified you are. It doesn't even matter if you adore what you do. What matters is that people know how to access you. Can people buy what you have? And do they know how to buy from you? Your marketing and sales are *not about you*, they're about your clients.

Marketing and sales are your selfless gift to the world. You're going to share what you do so that your future clients can benefit. Deliver outstanding client results to build your reputation. And you will scale your business while you sleep.

When you deliver what you say you will, you'll have a business built with integrity. You'll contribute fully. And stay at peace, knowing that you're keeping business true to your heart. A business built with integrity means no sleepless nights and lots of beauty sleep.

Remember, you're not going to sell your time. You'll produce ACE offers in a virtual framework. These irresistible packages support your quality clients. It's light-touch for you and high-return for your clients. Light-touch means that it's not labor intensive for you. It's results focused, not time based.

Your clients choose the package that's the best fit for the results they want. You'll give them the choice from your tiered offers.

Multiple Irresistible Offers

Repurpose your offers into a tiered model structure with multiple access points to you. The more access to you, the higher the price. The least access - like a free PDF download, the lower the cost. It's the same transformative information, repackaged. Tiered access levels position your ACE offers like delicious treats on a high-tea service tray. From lowest $0 to highest +$25000:

- Digital download (Guidebook / E-book / Journal)

- Value-packed information products (Cheatsheets, audits, assessments, swipe files)

- Challenge

- DIY course / Video training

- Online course

- Membership

- Multiple day events

- Group coaching

- One-on-one

- Accelerator program

- Mastermind

Packages

A package is a combination of multiple irresistible offers. For example:

Do it yourself - How to Create a Stand-out Style Guide for Social Media (self-study guidebook)

Done for you - Your Social Media Style Bible

Done with you - Stand Out 6-Week Online Course: Your Social Media Style, Revamped.

Combo - 3 Day Style Challenge. Including live training, support materials, and group support.

What support could you include into your package?

- Q &A sessions

- Email support

- Group accountability

- Bonuses (like information products)

Four quadrants of time and money

You'll customize your package based on the four quadrants of time and money. All your clients will fall into one of these four quadrants. Where they fall depends on which of your offers are right for them. Tiering your offers means that you can serve more than just the one type of income-generating client. You can build a future waitlist of clients.

#1 Not enough money and not enough time means you'll deliver quick-win, value-add freebies. These are your longer term prospects who you'll nurture until they're ready.

#2 Not enough money and enough time means you'll deliver high-impact training, workshops and challenges. These are great for case studies for new programs and courses.

#3 Enough money and not enough time means you'll deliver accelerator programs, VIP days or intensives, done for you packages and one-on-ones.

#4 Enough money and enough time means you'll deliver masterminds, private mentorships, and the best of your best packages.

#1 **NEM NET**	**#2** **NEM ET**
#3 **EM NET**	**#4** **EM ET**

Front end and back end packages

Your front-end package is your premium package that starts at $500 - $15000.

Your back-end package is your 10X version that is exclusive for graduates of your work only. For example, a $25,000 annual mentoring program (like I have for my most advanced program graduates).

Your back-end is for your clients who've already been through your ultimate front-end package. Brainstorm ideas for the 10X version of what you could give. This will give you fresh insights into creating your signature offers too.

For product based businesses your back-end offers would be custom and bespoke creations and collaborations for select clients only. The price point would be higher for original pieces.

The Over The Rainbow Strategy

From Problem to Promise

Abandoning the paradigm of problem-solution marketing opens you up to possibilities. You're released from the rhetoric of forceful shame and fear-based scarcity marketing. You start the conversation with the promise of where you finish.

This is The Over The Rainbow Strategy... where dreams come true. You're showing your future client a reality where their dreams have already come true. It's the "what happens next" part of the story. If your clients want the destination, they'll let you guide them to get there. You've painted a picture of something they want.

You want them to see, feel, touch and taste it. It needs to feel like a viable reality. The way to do that is to link the future dream reality to tangible real-life examples. We relate to specifics.

"Live a happy life" is generalized. How do you know you're living a happy life? What happens when you do?

If you said *"Go to bed smiling after a day fully spent"* you're adding a specific detail to the picture. You're saying happiness without saying happiness.

It's putting "Show to sell" into copywriting. It's based on the best creative writing advice, "Show, don't tell" by playwright, Anton Chekhov. You need to describe how the benefits of your business claim play out in their world. It's the classic how to do this...so that this happens. *"How to make your business your Sugar Daddy so that you can move to your beach house."*

The Over The Rainbow Strategy has a multi-level structure.

The overarching benefit of your business claim needs a name like Business Reimagined. That's what you'll get.

Next, you add a progression statement: from this to this. From patriarchal to playful business. Now you know the current reality and where you're going.

Then you'll have your unique process. This is how you'll guide your client through their transformational journey. Like, Business Alchemy.

Within your unique process, they'll arrive at certain milestones. These are your stages, secrets, or parts that make up the whole. I have Love, Play, and Magic inside Business Alchemy. The benefits you get from each of the stages are Impact, Income, and Interdependence.

How you get the benefits is what you'll do. Create your online persona, grow your connected community and scale your offers. You'll know you've done them because you'll have the benefit described. You'll have an online persona, a growing community and scaling offers. And when you do, you'll have a successful reimagined business to suit yourself.

This structure is magic because it shows the value of what you do without actually explaining how you do it. It entices your client to work with you to get the benefits. You're showing them the golden treasures without giving it all to them. You're showing them why they'd want it and what to expect on their journey to get it.

Most people offer their starting point as the solution. They say things like *"Have more time. Stress less. Lose weight. Make more money."* But they leave out what happens next. The Over The Rainbow Strategy says, *"that's just the beginning."* It holds the promise of so much more.

Have more time to take your kids on picnics.

Stress less to feel like a Zen- Buddhist monk - but in heels.

Lose weight to look like your top angel Instagram pic.

Make more money so you can lavish your loved ones with spontaneous presents.

Imagine that your solution is stage one. What comes next? And what's even better than that? Love, then play, then magic! Reimagine business to reimagine your entire life. Your business is just the first step to your Over The Rainbow life. Creating your treasures is playing all day. It's making your fantasies come to life.

The Over The Rainbow Strategy confirms that the dreams that you dream of really do come true. You've had to have been there to describe the details for someone who wants to get to where you're at.

The Over The Rainbow Strategy is how you master the messaging for your multiple irresistible offers.

Get

Reward yourself with the support you deserve. Up until this point, every single step has been set up for you to support others. Now it's your turn to get some sugar.

You know that you don't have do it all alone. It's about community, not competition and we are all better together. So, even though you could, you don't have to do it all by yourself. Celebrate your competence in collaboration with others instead of isolating yourself because of it. Virtual co-working is a great way to start.

Success leaves clues. Striking results are obvious. You can see who has succeeded already and you don't have to figure it all out on your own when they share their secrets. I call this the elevator path to success. With support, you get accountability to develop sustainable PLAY rhythms in flow with you. You save wasting time, money, and energy resources. You deserve to work with someone who has done it before. And most importantly, it's always more fun when you do it together! Who do you know who could show you how to reimagine your business?

Is it your partner? A simple accountability buddy? A coach? A mastermind group? An experienced mentor? Or say, I don't know, the prolific Creatrix whose book you're reading right now...who invites dream-makers into her Creative Business School? Could it really be that obvious? That black and white. Like the signs on the page and you're reading it right now? ... *that's up to you...*

Sistering

This book is dedicated to my sister because she's the best person I know. She coaches clarity and I coach creativity. It's the ultimate complementary combination. Because of her support, I learned how to support others. And how to celebrate their success. When I support her, I'm strengthened through the experience and vice versa. Sistering is literally the framework I use for my business support structure. And you're more than welcome to use it for yours too.

Sistering is a carpentry term. It refers to the secondary stud that is installed alongside the existing stud. Its purpose is to strengthen the load-bearing capacity of the structure. It becomes stronger, together through reinforcement. I love this term because it's exactly what having a sister feels like. A sister bears witness to your life, loves you unconditionally and supports you. That's what my relationship with my sister is like. Sistering is the ultimate example of an interdependent relationship between you and your future mentor.

Bounce-Back

The Bounce-Back strategy is so magical that I've even included it in the fairytale book I'm writing. In the fairytale version, it's how the lead character develops her magic skills. She bounces an iridescent bubble back and forth with her mentor. It grows bigger and more exquisite with each bounce. Magnified and more magnificent. Our business version is no less magical. It's real and that's even more magical than fantasy.

Bouncing an idea back and forth is a refinement process. Each Bounce-Back smooths and rounds out the idea until it's complete. It's able to roll out and gain momentum as it goes and grows. You start with an idea and bounce it to your mentor. They make a suggestion, challenge a premise, or highlight parts of the idea for you to expand, change or remove. You make the changes and bounce it back. If you're bouncing an idea in a group, you'll get collective input. The Bounce-Back is a collaborative process and the best masterminds do it.

It's up to you to take action and craft your idea. The Bounce-Back is a reflection on what's working best and what you can still improve.

Even the best ideas flourish in a Bounce-Back. There's only so much you can see from your perspective. Adding other viewpoints into the mix enriches your creation.

Recently a Creative Council Member shared her transition tagline with the Council. It was *"I help clients move from the mud to water."* She'd used a metaphor to explain their feeling state instead of an over used sentence like *"I help clients move from stuck to free."* But what she really offered was a deeper transformation than getting into a flow state. She's a life coach who specializes in transforming her clients' love lives and finances. She uses soul retrieval techniques that are an out of this world experience. Her clients make quantum leap changes. They realize they are their own soulmate and find their life partner in two years. She needed a name as powerful as her services.

"From your eye of the storm moment to sunshine days" was a Bounce-Back choice. But it still didn't give her a one-on-one program name. The Sunshine experience was generic and not specific enough. What she offered was more galaxy than world. More than time for a change, she promised transcendent transmutation. But using words like "transcendent transmutation" (as much as I love both words) is conceptual and not tangible enough. After completing the Bounce-Back process, she came up with: *The Venus Experience*. It spoke to the out-of-world experience, was intriguing yet relatable and expressed the promise of romantic living. It also said "this is for women" without saying "this is for women."

Whereas Free Flow can be done alone, the Bounce-Back needs another person to complete the process.

The Bounce-Back is an accelerated journey to The Over The Rainbow outcome. When I do three-month accelerators with individual clients, it's a heightened Bounce-Back intensive.

The Bounce-Back isn't getting feedback, it's integrating input to elevate the idea. It's similar to what we called *"Raising the stakes"* in playwriting class. You're creating a more potent, impactful version of what you started with.

You know you're close when your idea starts to feel exhilarating. It's more than just a promise for your client. It feels like a legacy creation for you.

Because you can't do it alone, you need to experience the Bounce-Back to integrate and comprehend it. If you want to get a feel for it, practice with this game. Imagine if your service or product cost ten times what it did now. If you offer a program for $500, imagine it cost $5000. What changes would you make to it, to make it worth $5000? What would you add, do differently and take away? Premium offers add exclusive, customized, and individual extras. They're not discounted for less.

One of my most successful clients had a collection of game reserves and safaris. He said that they never offered discounted or group prices for guests. Instead, they included once-in-a-lifetime experiences in the deal. They gave elephant interactions and private game drives in the deal. Add something special instead of discounting your price. Adding more of your time for less of a price is a time bundle. Don't do it. Instead imagine could you heighten and elevate the experience? What if the place your clients ended up at was their starting point. Where would they go next? This will give you an idea of what's possible when you Bounce-Back your idea with a creative business mentor. It's how you'd begin the Bounce-Back process.

In 2019 my private offer was Business Optimization. It's a super dry name and I was never in love with it. I was more excited about my Content Creators Council. Even though Business Optimization costs ten times the price. I developed the Business Optimization process into an art form. My clients delivered consistently outstanding results. They all made more money than they'd thought was possible. But the idea needed elevation to stay enticing. I realized that Business Optimization was only the starting point. The Over the Rainbow of Business Optimization is a Super Bloom business.

So I've created a VIP one-on-one accelerator program called Super Bloom your business. It's not about realizing that everything is figureoutable. My one-on-one clients are already capable, brilliant, and in a league of their own. It's about cultivating a flourishing business that demands attention. A magnificent business has a magical magnitude. It welcomes a community toward its warmth. It draws you in through its dynamic and resilient beauty.

Magical Technologies

The online world means you get to make money while you sleep. It's the ultimate light-touch approach because with the creative business structures in place, your business works for you - hands-free. You'll make your business virtually intelligent by setting up its framework online. This way you'll save time and money for your clients. And open yourself up to a global community with clients all around the world.

Money is not your most valuable currency - your time is. And not just your time but the quality of that time. You are constantly trading with it. And when you're doing too much, you will burn out. The faster you get results, the more time you have for your own creative expansion.

The world has changed. Virtualization became a COVID-19 prerequisite and is a great alternative option to meeting in person. Many people prefer meeting online. It's more convenient for both you and your clients. Virtualizing means to put it online. There are multiple ways to set up, support, and scale your business online.

Check out the bonus resource section for How to Virtualize Intelligently which also gives you access to my top tech-tools: **www.laurenwallett.com/biz-book**

Why you need a strategy first

Before we wrap up, I wanted to cover a pothole many of my clients have fallen into on their journey before success. They feel overwhelmed with their task list and so start hiring help and hemorrhaging money. They get a lot more done but little to no results to speak of. Hiring an assistant before having a strategy is like building a home without an architect or foundation. It's a disaster waiting to happen.

In reality, it's more work to do because you need to train and explain, teach, show and triple-check their work. Often, it's easier just to do it yourself. The idea of an assistant falls into the old business paradigm of "to be at the top, you need people underneath you." Except for the fact that - you don't. What you need is creative structure, support, and systems to scale you. Support gives you a solid foundation to build upon. Adding more people into existing chaos means more chaos. Hiring an assistant is about solving problems. Developing a creative business strategy is about creating solutions.

The thing is, you can solve all your problems and still not get what you actually want. In fact, you may end up solving problems that wouldn't have mattered when you're focused on what actually does.

Problems you may think you need to solve like:

- Building a website

- Getting a logo

- Figuring out your niche

- Having a specific target market

- Writing your "about page"

- Setting up a sales funnel

These are some of the last things to worry about and they're wasting your time. First, get clear on where you want to go instead of focusing on where you are now. That's why we start with your intention first and then reverse engineer the rest from there. Stop wasting time trying to make something that isn't even what you need function better. What you need is less quick fix and more upgrade only.

Hiring someone to help you within your current structure is just more work for you. A creative business strategy gives you a structural approach that you can build on. You can't build your dream home without an architect's blueprint. And you can't create a business reimagined without a creative business strategy. Once your structure is sound, you can absolutely outsource. But only when you know how it all fits together into the cohesive whole. Otherwise, it becomes more of a tangled mess. Support gives you the strength to scale.

Return to your drawing board and map out your strategy before you delegate and hire. And better still, Bounce-Back your plan with an experienced creative business mentor. That'll ensure you've filled all the gaps and maximized all your opportunities. You have nothing to lose and everything to gain.

P.S: *Every successful person you've ever heard of has had help to get where they are.*

Business Mentor Checklist

A great business mentor:

Combines coaching, consulting, mentorship and guidance

Treats you as a unique creator (NOT a ticket to close/typical client in a box)

Offers robust support and accountability

Has an excellent track record and background

Shares amazing client results

Gives transparent pricing

Interdependence Success

From overwhelmed to optimized

She was the kind of person who could do it all and so she constantly bit off more than she could chew. When we started, she was an Olympic Athlete who ran a global events company. She was overwhelmed with the volume of work that needed to be done. Highly efficient, effective, and capable, she took on too much work herself. She had no systems in place to scale.

She wanted a more relaxed lifestyle but with every success, she made more money and lost more time. Her balance was off. She needed to realign to her true values. And prioritize her lifestyle without losing success. She thought she needed to hire more people and squeeze more into her day. But what she needed was systems and structure that enabled time out.

In the beginning she was:

- Accepting every new event

- Selling multiple products and services

- Wanting to expand her personal brand

She made strategic decisions about what events she'd deliver. She prioritized the highest return financially and energetically and let go of all opportunities that were actually burdens.

We set up a virtual drawing board to map out and streamline her systems. We simplified her services and created the structure to scale. She optimized her community to market and promote her events for her. And most importantly, she gave herself the support of an experienced creative business mentor.

We bounced ideas back, put a team in place, and got the right tech tools to scale. She outlined her processes, defined scopes of work, and with a sound structure, had more time for new creative pursuits. She got her lifestyle back.

Beyond the book

Take Action

You're read about how to birth your business and discovered the ingredients needed for Business Alchemy. Now it's time to take action. Magic is yours for the making! Beyond the book gives you support for your business creation and expansion. You have everything you need and all that it takes to reimagine your business.

I'm celebrating your success from the future!

Quality Client Check

You're not for everyone, and everyone isn't for you. I don't do demographics for potential clients and don't advise you do them either. Business Reimagined allows your clients to come to you through magnetic attraction. If you do one-on-one or group work, here's a shortlist to keep in mind. You want to reach the ultimate goal: resonant referrals.

Double Delight

Clients you can really make a difference with and who you love to work with. Every client you take on requires an energetic exchange. Don't take on clients who drain and deplete you. Audition your clients before you accept them.

No Credit Card Clients

Quality clients aren't flat broke. They understand the importance of investment and are willing to pay to get the results they want. They don't have to use their credit card to afford to work with you.

Recurring Fee

They either enter long term programs with you or buy again and again. They're not a once-off "ticket" that you close. (Beware of anyone who calls a client a ticket.)

Referral

They resonate with you and have the results to share, so they refer you to others. And because you now know their excellence, you're able to refer them to your network. It goes both ways.

Remember, systematic racism, misogyny, sexism, heterosexism, and ableism means that not everyone has had the same opportunity to make money. To make your business more inclusive, you can absolutely offer:

- A sliding scale

- Discounts

- Scholarships

- Awards

You don't have to advertise this and can do it at your own discretion. When I met a client with potential, who isn't yet financially able, I offer alternative prices. But I don't convince someone who has no money to take out a loan to work with me.

Resonance gets referrals

Interconnected

I was born in South Africa where we have a beautiful word: Ubuntu. It's an African way of living that translates to, "I am because we are". We are all interconnected. And I run The Creative Business School with this in mind.

When I met one of my first American clients, she was living in a ground floor one-bedroom apartment. She earned $5000 per month. After working together, she started selling packages starting from $5000 and ranging to $50000. Within a year, she'd moved into a three-story house she bought! I went to visit her during the final walk-through of her home and I met her real estate agent. She told him what I'd done for her and he hired me on the spot.

He was driven, passionate, and strove for excellence in everything he did, so I introduced him to my client, a Hollywood PR coach and she got him a live TV interview about his service style. I introduced the Hollywood PR coach to another quality client of mine, an outstanding Life Coach and they started working together.

My community of clients is supportive, connected, and leverages one another through their own personal networks.

I carefully choose who to work with because I introduce clients into my community. It's a luxury and a treat to meet my network of VIP clients so I audition potential clients before I agree to mentor them.

Success Stories

For dozens of success stories, visit
www.laurenwallett.com/apply
And hear it straight from my clients in their own words.

Business Check list:

Do you have these three elements?

- A Captivating Online Persona

- A Thriving Community

- Multiple Scalable Offers

If you had to give each section a color:

- *Green:*   I've got it completely covered. It's a go!

- *Orange:*   I could use some help. I've sort of got this.

- *Red:*   I need some urgent support. I don't get this.

R I C H Deep Dive

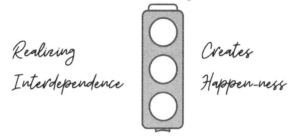

Realizing
Interdependence

Creates
Happen-ness

Red -   **I need some urgent help.
I don't get this.**

Orange -   **I could use some help.
I've sort of got this.**

Green -   **I've got full support. It's
a go!**

R.I.C.H Deep Dive:

What have you already made happen?

Answer these 7 questions to see where you're at and what needs to happen next.

#1 I know my content genius and am playing to my strengths with a compelling creative strategy

Red / Orange / Green

#2 I've packaged premium services and products into packages instead of selling time bundles

Red / Orange / Green

#3 My online community grows every week

Red / Orange / Green

#4 I have a waitlist of clients

Red / Orange / Green

#5 My outstanding results mean I'm earning more and working less

Red / Orange / Green

#6 I only do my favorite parts of my business and the rest is outsourced

Red / Orange / Green

#7 I have the best support and am scaling my business

Red / Orange / Green

If you're green in every section, congratulations!

If there are some orange and reds, then check out the resources section: **www.laurenwallett.com/biz-book**

After

After I decided to rewrite this book from "How to make your business your Sugar Daddy so you can move to your beach house" into Love, Play, Magic : Business Reimagined, this happened...

Writing about my previous businesses reminded me how much I love creating business. I've remembered so many businesses I didn't mention:

The Coffee Cushion Collection of cushions, ottomans, and lampshades

A steel and wood furniture collection (tables, stools, and cheese boards)

Bunny Girl (ceramic rabbits shipped on the full moon)

Two frame collections (vintage and custom "Ideas in Boxes")

And many more...

I missed how fun product businesses were. So I decided to start up a new business. I'd written the ultimate business playbook, so I held the "How To" guide in my hand! I set up and launched a candle collection called Burn it Down Candles. The launch was on the 11th February 2021, the new moon in Aquarius. I took all my advice on Love, Play, and Magic and launched online. It's already growing like wildfire!

Writing this book changed my life.
I hope it changes yours too.

Resources

For complimentary resources to each section of this book, visit:
www.laurenwallett.com/biz-book

Blogs

Want more? Subscribe to my blog for weekly Biz Love notes.
www.laurenwallett.com/blog

Book Sound Track

Have you ever read to a soundtrack? It's one of my favorite things to do. So I've made you this business inspired soundtrack on Spotify. Click here:
https://open.spotify.com/playlist/5USWTUBHLV6gbC15jid3tA? si=9c74a8408dbd4e5c

A click-through link is also at **www.laurenwallett.com/biz-book**

About Lauren Wallett

In the three years I've lived in Los Angeles I've experienced exponential growth in both my business and lifestyle. I live a delicious, wildly romantic, and enchanted life. In October 2020, I moved into my Hermosa Beach home. When I'm not drinking Mochas, watching sunsets, singing and dancing in my bikini, planting in my robe or taking a rose petal bubble baths, I'm writing books and fairytales. I'm currently writing the origin story of the Fairy Godmother to reveal the hidden truth about a legendary lie. I get to do what I love each and every single day.

For my personal adventures, connect with me
@laurenwallett on Instagram
and
@lauren.wallett on TikTok
Tag me @laurenwallett in pictures with this book!

And for more visit
www.laurenwallett.com

www.laurenwallett.com

Enjoy playing all day

Love, Lauren

Made in United States
North Haven, CT
29 April 2022

18719100R00108